"Rose Marie Miller's new book is a beautiful trifecta of weakness, faith, and power. Rose Marie seamlessly embeds her writing with these three themes, not through cleverness and willful intent, but rather through the spiritual stealth that only God at work in a person can achieve. This is why I love Rose Marie and read her work. She is a broken soul given over to the renewing love of her Maker. There's no artifice here—it's all heart."

Charlie Peacock, Cofounder, Art House America; record producer

"I've heard great sermons on nothing being impossible with God; I've seen those words from Jesus needle-pointed, done in calligraphy, and written out on three-by-five cards and taped to the front of refrigerators. But there is one person in my forty-five years of knowing the Lord who has been a living validation of this promise, more so than anyone else, and that is Rose Marie Miller, my spiritual mom. That's why I am thrilled with her new book. Hype-free, spin-free gospel sanity is the best way I know to describe Rose Marie's new book. It you want to know how the fragrance of the gospel is released through those who have the courage to own their brokenness and weakness, this is your book."

Scotty Smith, Founding Pastor, Christ Community Church; author of *Everyday Prayers: 365 Days to a Gospel-Centered Faith*

"Thank you, Rose Marie, for your powerful words that challenge me to know forgiveness and to forgive, to rest in Jesus when I am weak and desperate, and to persevere in prayer. You met your goal for this book: perhaps I am finally ready to grow in that counterintuitive life in which I spend more time with Jesus when days are especially hectic."

Edward T. Welch, PhD, CCEF Faculty; licensed psychologist; author of *Shame Interrupted*

"With characteristic humility and warmth, Rose Marie Miller has written a book sweet with the love of Christ on every page. This is a very personal reflection on how God's grace continues to unfold in her life through repentance, forgiveness, prayer, and faith. You'll feel like you're meeting with a dear friend who both knows your heart and, most importantly, the heart of our Savior."

Winston T. Smith, CCEF Faculty; author of *Marriage Matters*

"At World Harvest Mission, Rose Marie is affectionately known as our spiritual mother. Over the years she has consistently challenged us to a life of dependent prayer where you realize how great and wonderful God's promises are when you dare to pray boldly. On behalf of all of us at World Harvest, I highly commend this book to you—expect to be changed and blessed as we have by Rose Marie's ministry to us!"

Bob Osborne, Executive Director, World Harvest Mission

Nothing Is Impossible with God

REFLECTIONS ON WEAKNESS, FAITH, AND POWER

Rose Marie Miller

New Growth Press

New Growth Press, Greensboro, NC 27404
www.newgrowthpress.com
Copyright © 2012 by Rose Marie Miller.

Cover Design: Faceout Books, faceoutbooks.com
Interior Design and Typesetting: North Market Street Graphics

ISBN 978-1-936768-68-4
ISBN 978-1-936768-57-8 (ebook)

Library of Congress Cataloging-in-Publication Data
Miller, Rose Marie, 1924–
Nothing is impossible with God : reflections on weakness, faith, and power /
Rose Marie Miller.
p. cm.
Includes bibliographical references (p.   ) and index.
ISBN-13: 978-1-936768-68-4 (alk. paper)
ISBN-10: 1-936768-68-2 (alk. paper)
1. God (Chrisianity)—Omnipotence. 2. Spiritual life—Christianity. I. Title.
BT133.M55 2012
248.4—dc23   2012016596

Printed in Canada

19 18 17 16 15 14 13 12   1 2 3 4 5

FOREWORD

My mom has written a great book on her life's journey since Dad's homegoing in 1996. But the best book is the one I get to watch every day—her life. Paul tells the Corinthians, "You show that you are a letter from Christ" (2 Corinthians 3:3). I love to tell people, "How many 87-year-old women work almost full time as missionaries to Hindus in London?" When she is in London—when weddings or births or visa problems aren't pulling her home—she is regularly serving and meeting with Asian woman. She just loves it.

But it gets better. Mom is not just working in London; she communicates regularly with her family of five children, twenty-four grandchildren, and twenty great-grandchildren. Just getting birthday presents for that horde is a full-time job in itself.

And better. She reads voraciously. She introduced me to the genre of British Indian fiction some years ago. I didn't even know what the Man Booker Prize was until Mom said to me, "Paul, you need to read *Brick Lane*; it was just short-listed for the Man Booker Prize." The what? How many middle-aged sons are kept on the cutting edge of culture by their moms?

And still better. Mom has cultivated about a dozen, maybe even a couple of dozen friendships with women who share their lives with her and she with them. One of those friends, Sandy Elder, said this about Mom, "My friend Shirley and I often say, no matter the age difference—in our case thirty years—she is our peer. What we mean by that is that whatever we confess to her that we are struggling with, she has this amazing way of responding, 'Oh ladies, believe me, I struggle with the same thing in my heart too, so please pray for me as I pray for you.' And we know she does. She is also one of the few women I know who has made the Holy Spirit real and accessible through her testimonies and teaching; it is, I suppose, because she really does rely on Christ through the Spirit."

And for those of you who are familiar with the Sonship course, Mom is constantly rediscovering the gospel. She will battle out of a fog into the clear air of the love of God for her. Her spirits will lift when something from the Word feeds her soul. Another friend, Sandy Smallman, said this about Mom, "I am always challenged and blessed by Rose Marie's 'restless' Christian heart—restless in a good way. She is never willing to simply be a status quo Christian, one who is happy with some blessings here and there. She demands more. She wants more of God, more participation in his ministry, more of his peace and joy. She frequently asks me to pray that she would not depart from a simple and pure devotion to Christ. She says that so often that it has become something like a mantra to me. She often adds that she prays that for me as well."

Mom has sown a life immersed in the Word, and she is reaping a harvest of faith. All our lives have trajectories; all of us are in a continuing process of reaping and sowing. Old age, though, is heavily weighted toward the reaping side of life. It is the time in life when, to quote Jesus, "hidden things are revealed." If I had to summarize Mom's life I would say, "In the battle of life, she immersed herself in the Word and community, which in turn fed her faith and empowered her love." Easy to say. Wicked hard to do. She often tells me the back story of what is going on in her life. Mom's life now is characterized by ongoing forgiveness, surrendering her will, waiting on God, fighting discouragement, and just everyday, ordinary stuff.

Mom's example has impacted my wife Jill's assessment of my retirement: Jill informed me that it wasn't going to happen! It was a no-brainer for Jill. She compared Mom's life with the lives of Christians who slowed down and drifted into low-level narcissism, and she didn't want any part of it. The life of a pilgrim is far too attractive. Proverbs captures it best, "The path of the righteous is like the light of dawn, which shines brighter and brighter until full day" (Proverbs 4:18).

So why tell you all this? Someone once said that the secret to reading John Piper's books was to hear him preaching the book as you read them. Then it would come alive. Well the secret to reading Rose Marie's book is to see her living what she is saying. So when she encourages you to believe (since this book is all about faith), remember this is a believing woman. When she encourages you to pray, remember this is a praying woman. So enjoy the book. Learn from the book. (It will feed your faith.) Enjoy watching Mom reap. Enjoy the trajectory of her life. Just remember that the real book is working in London with Hindu women.

Paul E. Miller
www.APrayingLife.com

ACKNOWLEDGMENTS

Four years ago, I began thinking about writing a book comprised of talks, meditations, lectures, and reflections on how God has been with me on the journey of life. I asked seven women to pray for this undertaking. Thank you Andi, Diane, Betsy, Carolyn, Sandy, Holly, and Jan. You prayed, bore my burdens, and believed that God had taught me lessons that should be shared.

To my daughter Barbara and son-in-law Angelo, who faithfully cared for my sister so that I could be in London. The burdens were heavy and you bore them with enduring love. Thank you from my heart.

To Sue Lutz, my editor. Who else could take all the material I gave you and shape it into a readable book! Thank you for believing that what God taught—and you helped reshape—would be an encouragement to God's people.

To Jan Powers, my assistant. What would I have done without your careful eye for detail, your expertise on the computer, and your heart for this endeavor even in the last week of your mother's life? You sat by her bedside and still faithfully gave of your time to meet a deadline.

To Bob Osborne, director of World Harvest Mission, and the Sending Center team, who prayed, encouraged, and believed that I could be effective in London at age 86 and even write a book that would encourage others.

To my Indian friends in Southall, who have been my teachers, helping me to make great truths simple, understandable, and applicable. You are a reminder that, in the hardships of life, Jesus is the only answer. You invited me into your life, calling me Mum and Grandmum.

To my beloved family: Roseann, Ruth, Paul, Barbara, and Keren and their spouses, twenty-four grandchildren, seventeen great-grandchildren and counting! I treasure you though I do not see you as much as I would like. You are kingdom builders. I know you pray.

To my "special needs" granddaughter, Kimberly Rose Marie Miller, who prays for me every day. Thank you, Kim. I still need your prayers.

Last but not least, thanks to the hundreds of people who faithfully prayed, encouraged, and gave. You did so from your hearts.

Rose Marie Miller, July 4, 2011

To my sister Barbara. We miss her joy in simple things and her faithful prayers.

TABLE OF CONTENTS

A Garden Locked Up

Nothing is impossible with God. I had always heard this, but for a long time it didn't seem to be true for me. For much of my life I kept God at a distance, building walls of self-protection and self-reliance. I said I was a Christian but my life said, "I can manage without God." When crises came, the walls went higher.

But there came a day when building walls did not work and I was left with, "I don't believe God exists, or if he does exist, he is a dark cloud over my life—a cloud of fear, guilt, condemnation, and loneliness." Into this dark cloud God spoke, not with an audible voice, but with life-giving words.

God, for whom nothing really is impossible—not even changing a self-righteous, independent, desperately-trying-to-keep-it-all-together pastor's wife—gave me himself.

In the early 1970s, my husband, Jack, a pastor and seminary professor, was asked to teach on discipleship to a group of people who wanted to know how "it" worked. The site for the lecture was an auditorium about an hour's drive from our home. Feeling a sense of duty toward Jack, and since we had a guest staying with us, I went along reluctantly. Normally, the drive through rural Bucks County was beautiful, so I looked forward to that. But the trip was spoiled for me not only because of my attitude but because the person driving with us did nothing but talk about himself. By the time we arrived, I was seriously annoyed. I was not ready for God to teach me anything.

The building was old, typical for the area, with tiers of white painted cement benches. I decided to sit near the top, away from most of the people. I had already decided that I wouldn't learn anything useful anyway, and I wanted to be alone.

In that moment of discontent, these words quietly and gently came to my mind: "A garden locked is my sister, my bride, a rock garden locked, a spring sealed up" (Song of Solomon 4:12 NASB). My first thought was, "Where did that come from?" Looking in my Bible's concordance I found the verse in the Song of Solomon.

My mind was captured by the thought of a garden locked up. I thought back through my life to all the times I had felt that way—locked up. My parents were immigrants from Germany. Learning to live in a foreign land where everything was different, losing hard-earned money in the Depression, and dealing with the challenges of raising my mentally challenged sister had left my mother bitter. Over time, the burdens overwhelmed her, and in desperation she tried to take her own life. One day when I was about thirteen years old, I was alone in the house with my mother when I smelled gas. I ran into the kitchen and saw her head in the oven. With fear gripping my heart, I turned off the gas, pulled her away from the stove, and opened all the windows. My voice shook with tears as I called my dad at his garage in San Francisco and told him to come home.

From that day on, my dad and I never talked about what had happened, but it was our unspoken pact that we would do whatever we had to do to keep my mother in the home and keep her from taking her life. The fact that I couldn't talk about what was happening locked up my emotions. I knew something was seriously wrong but did not know how to express my feelings. I decided to write my mother a note, which I left on the kitchen table. Strangely, I do not remember what I wrote. My mother showed it to my father who sternly asked me why I had written it. I lied and said, "I was trying out my pencil. I didn't mean what I wrote." My father was angry and my mother was hurt. It was many years before I again risked expressing my feelings. Soon my mother showed classic signs of schizophrenia. Again, this was not something my dad and I talked about. Not knowing how to deal with the shame of the situation, I insulated myself from my emotions reasoning that what I didn't feel wouldn't hurt me.

These were the memories that flooded my mind as I continued to read from the Song of Solomon that day in Bucks County. "Your shoots are an orchard of pomegranates with choice fruits, henna with nard plants, nard and saffron, calamus and cinnamon, with all the trees of frankincense, myrrh and aloes, along with all the finest spices" (Song of Solomon 4:13–14 NASB).

I wondered if Solomon's words described me. Was I a locked garden full of spices and choice fruits? Could I be, in reality, "a garden spring, a well of fresh water" (4:15 NASB)? Everything this garden needed to flourish was provided. Was God giving me a picture of my life? It didn't seem possible.

Only a handful of times have I known for certain that God was speaking into the core of my heart. This was one of them. I sat on that bench, a dissatisfied, self-righteous failure—so many painful emotions locked up inside me. I knew that God was unlocking the gate, so to speak, to show me a whole new picture of myself. Where I saw rotten fruit and weeds, he saw fruit and spices. Where I saw mud and sludge; he saw a fountain, a well of fresh water, and flowing streams.

Quiet joy began to make its way into my soul. Yes, the winds would blow, but the spices would also flow. "Awake, O north wind, and come, O south wind! Blow upon my garden, let its spices flow" (4:16 ESV). From my place of discouragement, I was about to learn that nothing is impossible with God.

For the spices to flow out of the garden, the north wind had to blow. And blow it did in the years that followed, to the point where I often lost sight of the plan and purpose of God. But then the gentle south wind would come, giving me courage to continue after the storms.

The passage ends with, "May my beloved come into his garden and eat its choice fruits!" (4:16 NASB). There would be many times in the years ahead when I would resist God's advances, but when he would finally come in—as he always would—the fruit would ripen, the spices mature, and the water run clean.

What God began to teach me that day was that he had a heart for me. He knew me in a way I did not know myself. He saw me in a way I did not see myself. There was a lot more beauty and hope in his perspective than in mine.

This book tells how God nurtured me and matured me in the years that followed—how he did the impossible in me. It's a collection of personal meditations, journal entries, talks, and Bible studies that I have written over the years. Together they illustrate what my Beloved Jesus has done in my heart and life. When God began to unlock the garden of my heart, he invited me to join in his mission to make this broken world an inheritance for his Son. His assignments haven't been easy, but I love and trust my Gardener and I am filled with joy to partner with him. He truly is the God of the impossible.

Perhaps like me, you know many true things about God but don't really know him or taste the fruit of the garden he has planted in your heart. I invite you to let the Lord unlock your heart too. May the things God has taught me flow into your life and encourage you to let the Consummate Gardener come and do the impossible in you.

Rediscovering
the Gospel

When God met me in the last row of that small auditorium, I did not realize the implications of the "north wind" blowing. I just knew that God understood me. But God knew that I needed the truth of who he is to become the center of my life. He is the God for whom nothing is impossible—I needed to know this. At the time, my life was centered on self: what I could and could not do. I was focused on my own kingdom building. I did not understand that it is all about God and his kingdom. In the years that followed, God dismantled my strength. He patiently tore down walls of approval seeking, blame shifting, demanding peace on my terms, and retreating from conflict. He enlarged my heart to believe and trust in his plan, not only for my life and family, but also for his bigger purpose of displaying his glory among the nations.

In the early 1970s, the Spirit was already working in Jack's life. He was gripped in a powerful way by his own sin and the power of the gospel to renew him daily. This led to a decision in 1973 to plant New Life Presbyterian Church. Six years later, it led to a ministry trip to Uganda. We had been invited there by a church leader who had fled the country during Idi Amin's reign and had worshiped at New Life. Once he returned home, he asked us to come to help restore the church and the country.

The Lord blessed the trip in powerful and exciting ways. When we returned to the United States with the good news of what God was doing, many young people wanted to return with us. But Jack realized that a zeal for mission would only go so far. He told those who were eager to go with him, "You will encounter depravity in others and in yourself. The only cure is the power of the gospel. It must grip your heart."

Jack began to teach these individuals what they would need spiritually for such a task. The emphasis was on living as sons and daughters of God, rather than as orphans. As our son, Paul, listened to the talks, he developed them into a series we later called "Sonship." A discipling and mentoring course was born.

What you are about to read are the three talks I typically gave in the Sonship course in its early years. I gave my testimony, talked about forgiveness as a lifestyle, and shared the importance of a clean conscience before God. I include them to introduce you to what I learned during those years, which laid the foundation for everything that has happened since.

No one ever arrives at a place where old sin patterns do not return, but what Sonship emphasizes is that growth in grace is possible when sin is acknowledged, confessed, and by grace, forsaken. As I have discovered, it is a beginning that God uses to send us out into the world with the purpose of exalting him among the nations. I hope these talks will encourage you to let the Consummate Gardener continue his work in your own heart.

1

My Testimony

⁓

If you had told me years ago that I would be speaking about living in the freedom of the gospel, I would have laughed. I grew up in a family that knew very little about freedom and a lot about control. My parents were German immigrants, and the most significant aspect of our lives was the fact that my mother was a paranoid schizophrenic. She accused every visitor to our house of being a spy, so people stopped coming. When we went out to dinner, she accused other diners of spying on her. Our family became lonely and isolated, focused on keeping my mother from taking her own life. I believed in God during those years, but I wasn't sure he was particularly concerned about our problems. I believed that Jesus came to die for sinners, but since I didn't see myself as much of a sinner, that didn't have much of an effect on me.

Still, I always went to church on Sunday, and that is where I met my husband, Jack. When we married, I was freed from the daily burden of caring for my mother. Jack's enthusiastic faith introduced me to God's personal care over our lives. For the first time, I felt safe. God was good.

A LIFE OF LEGALISM

These changes were a dramatic departure from what I had known at home, but in many ways I was unchanged from the girl I had been. Jack was so excited about Jesus and the power of the gospel that he didn't realize that the gospel was not *my* working theology. Mine was moralism and legalism—a religion of duty, rules, and self-control through human willpower. The goal was self-justification, not the justification by faith in Christ that the gospel offers. But, as many people can tell you, moralism and legalism can "pass" for Christianity, at least outwardly, in the good times. It is only when crises come that you find there is no foundation on which to stand. And crises are what God used to reveal my heart's true need for him.

As God worked in Jack's life, he immersed himself more and more in ministry. I had thought I was marrying a future college professor, but then Jack decided to become a minister. In fact he became a pastor, church planter, seminary professor, and evangelist. He always wanted me to be involved with him in ministry, and dutifully I tried to comply. But it was superficial compliance, and all the heart struggles I did not express brought an underlying resentment to my relationship with Jack and with God.

The crisis came in the early seventies. God did a work of renewal in Jack's life, and he was filled with boundless confidence that the gospel could change *anybody*. As a fruit of that conviction, we began to take troubled young people into our big, old three-story house in the outskirts of Philadelphia. These people were in desperate need: drug addicts, refugees, state hospital dropouts, and former members of motorcycle gangs. We saw some dramatic conversions, and from this work sprang the seeds that blossomed into New Life Presbyterian Church.

Jack's role in our ministry to these troubled people was to be the representative of grace. He gave the gospel to everyone in the house. I was the law, motherly but firm and resolute. It was needed. Some of these people were really burdened and it took firm measures to keep them under control. During this time, however, I was a growing puzzle to my husband. He would tell me how gifted I was and how effective my work was becoming, but it only made me feel guilty. I should say even *more* guilty because there was a dark cloud over my life. Even the beautiful conversions taking place in our home and the new lives developing did not give me lasting joy. No matter how well things went for me, I always felt I should have done more. I could see countless flaws in the best things I did. In fact, my private view of myself was that I never could do anything really worthwhile.

I remember an experience that typified my attitude. In the sixties, Jack received annual invitations to speak at "Skis and Skeptics" evangelistic weekends in the Pocono Mountains. Jack approached the events with typical enthusiasm, earnestly seeking to win every skeptic to Christ. Me? I loved the skiing and at night slipped up to my room with my favorite Agatha Christie novel under my coat. While Jack fought for the lives of the skeptics downstairs in the lodge, I unraveled the mysteries of Agatha snuggled under the covers. Only skiing and Agatha made these weekends bearable. Actually, I used to pray that no money would come in so that I would not have to go. Nowhere in me could I find the wisdom and compassion needed to reach out to these college students. I felt that I didn't have anything to offer anyone. I felt as if I barely knew Christ as a real person myself. The more I thought about it, the more I was paralyzed. What to say? How to say it? When to say it? And then afterward, Did I say it right?

It was hard to get Jack to hear how I felt. I often complained to him, "You don't listen." But all I gave him to listen to were problems—my own and those of the people who lived with us. Worse yet, I expected Jack to act as Holy Spirit and solve these problems for me. I expected Jack to make the people who lived with us holy, and I expected him to make me happy. Jack, for his part, didn't listen to the deeper struggles of my heart. The pressure built inside me until July 1974 when we vacationed in Tennessee. Walking by the lake one evening, I blurted, "I feel like I am walking under a dark cloud. God seems far away, and I don't even know if I believe he exists." Up to this point Jack usually had had ready answers, but now he was shocked into silence.

ANOTHER RIGHTEOUSNESS

As soon as we returned home, Jack handed me a copy of the introduction to Martin Luther's commentary on Galatians. I read, "For in the righteousness of faith . . . we work nothing, we render nothing unto God, but we only receive, and suffer another to work in us, that is to say, God."[1] I was ready to hear about another righteousness that was available to me. At that time we had living with us a charming, cultured young man who continually evaded and resisted our efforts to get him to take responsibility in the home. I could forgive the living illustrations of Romans 1 that we had taken in before, but I couldn't forgive this fellow's expectations that we serve him hand and foot. I couldn't love him. Legalism can go a long way, but it can't help you love. I saw that I hated my circumstances and the people I couldn't control. I felt so guilty, and I would have loved to have someone give me the desire and power to love, but I didn't know what I had to do to get it.

I kept reading Martin Luther and a year later, during a conference in Switzerland, the Lord made it clear what I needed to do. Jack was speaking at a conference on family relationships and I chose one sunny day to go skiing. I chose the mountain, too—one that was way beyond my skill as a skier. Ten feet from the top I fell and lost one ski. Although I could have turned right around and gone down the mountain on the gondola, I did not. For two hours I slid and bumped and fell down that mountain. When I got back to the hotel, weary and aching, I slid into a hot tub. Typically (for me), I responded by being angry at God. Wasn't it his fault that I had made such a fool of myself? After all, he knew how high that mountain was. He could have kept me from going.

But the Lord had something better to cover me with than all my ready excuses. Sunday morning during a Communion service, Jack broke a large loaf of French bread to pass around. In the crack of that bread, I suddenly saw Jesus broken for me. My moralism, pride, and self-righteousness were exposed and covered at the same time. Finally I understood what Luther was saying: that Jesus' righteousness covered all my unrighteousness. What did I need to do to get it? Just accept his work for me. As I sat there with tears streaming down my face and one small tissue to stem the tide, I saw my trip down the mountain as a dismal picture of my record of self-righteousness and self-sufficiency. I was struck by the obvious fact that I hadn't needed to go down the mountain the way I had. I could have enjoyed a cup of tea in the mountaintop restaurant and gone down on the gondola, admitting that for me skiing down was an impossibility. I suddenly saw my past as so much self-effort that had produced "good things" but could not deal with failure or defeat. Now I understood that I could turn to Christ and ask for forgiveness, and his righteousness would cover all of that. All my excuses were gone, and I accepted Christ's perfect record as what I needed. All my self-righteousness made me a spiritual paralytic, but Christ's righteousness brought peace, healing, and restoration. God reached into my life and dealt with my fundamental sin.

Before this, my way of thinking had been centered on moral failure and success, not sin and grace. I thought of sin as a social failure on my part or on others.' I felt condemned by these failures, but I defended myself by blaming others when things didn't go the way I wanted. And then I tried to clear my conscience by getting busy with work and duty. I always wanted God to strengthen my strength and enhance my good record. But now I saw that though I could not love, Christ had loved *for* me. The only worthwhile record was Christ's record, his obedient life and his death for my sins. Until then, I had never seen, let alone admitted, that I had neither strength nor righteousness of my own. But now I brought my real sins to a real Savior, and I was forgiven. I knew that I was loved unconditionally by a holy, righteous God. What a marvelous relief God's grace in Christ offered! For the first time, my heart was at peace with God and I was at peace with myself.

When we returned home, the message of justification by faith began to give me purpose and identity in my marriage and ministry with Jack. I knew we were partners together in the gospel. I could speak with conviction about the power of the gospel to dispel the dark clouds of guilt that hang over our lives: it had done this for me. I began to study the book of Galatians in earnest.

When we took a day off, my conversation was no longer filled with my problems. Now I had things to share with Jack about how Galatians applied to my needs and to the needs of those around me.

THE GOSPEL IN UGANDA

In December, 1979, Jack received an invitation from a Ugandan pastor, a former student at Westminster Seminary, to minister to the church in Uganda as it emerged from the bloody violence of Idi Amin's eight-year reign of terror. Jack prepared to go with his usual enthusiasm, and I prepared with fear. I was sure I was going to die; I was just praying that it would be a quick bullet to my head. God was still molding this team!

For several months we stayed in Kampala in a hotel filled with returning exiles, Asians, and Indians. We made friends and prayed with people of all religions through one crisis after another, including insecurity, sickness, loneliness, bad food, and no water. During this time we saw more evil than we had in twenty-three years of ministry. The physical and emotional brutality wore away at my soul. I did not know how to handle all the evil I heard about and saw. My heart was heavy and unsettled, loveless and numb.

I was brought back to reality by another Communion service, this time at a church whose windows had been bombed out during the war. As I sat there wondering if I could ever love the Ugandan people, the answer came again as the bread broke. I was reminded once more of how much I needed God's forgiveness for my faithless, loveless response to what I was seeing. As I took the bread and the cup, his forgiveness filled my heart.

This is always the answer, but I was so quick to forget. Later we stopped at a small mud hut to share the Lord's Supper with an elderly Ugandan widow. She had lost her husband and ten sons under Amin's reign. But there was no complaining, only a sweet love for Jesus. She was a living example to me of God's grace and forgiveness.

But I still had much to learn about relying on God's grace. On our way home from Uganda, we went to Kenya for two weeks of rest. We went to Mombasa, a fashionable resort for Africans, Asians, and Europeans. Our overnight train trip felt like a honeymoon as we awakened to a porter bringing us tea and glimpsed a giraffe outside our window. But for me the mood was shattered on our first evening there. We went with some missionaries to a small park overlooking the Indian Ocean. I was content to rest and enjoy the beauty of the scene, but with us in the park were many Muslims meeting to enjoy friendships and the balmy evening air. Jack and some of the missionaries began to preach, and soon I heard him say, "My wife will now tell you how a Christian marriage works." All the beauty of the evening was gone for me. But submission out of duty took me to where the others were speaking. I spoke reluctantly and later was overwhelmed with a deep sense of guilt, despair, and defeat. Anger and resentment smoldered in me.

AN ORPHAN OR A DAUGHTER?

On the way home, Jack and I stopped for a few days in Switzerland, the place where God had met me earlier and a place I love because of the beautiful mountains and the order and cleanliness of the culture. But even that did not bring rest to my spirit because the

Holy Spirit was at work, waiting to teach me something new. As we walked the streets of Geneva, surrounded by sophisticated, well-dressed people, I finally couldn't hold it in any longer. My suppressed anger and guilt came to the surface. With tears streaming down my cheeks I said to Jack, "Why couldn't I cope? Why do I collapse so often and then get filled with guilt? What is wrong with me?" Jack turned to me and said, "Rose Marie, you act like an orphan. You act as if the Holy Spirit never came and could never help you through impossible situations like Uganda and Mombasa. You act as if there is no Father who loves you."

The Holy Spirit took those words and pressed them into my heart. I knew Jack was right. All I could say was, "Lord, I am sorry. Please teach me how to be a daughter." In Uganda I had seen lots of orphans. One had tried to steal my purse as we knelt to pray in the marketplace. They would kill almost as quickly as steal. Because they had no father to look after them, they made sure they took care of themselves by lying, cheating, stealing, and deceiving to get along. I had been acting like them—as if I had no father, as if I didn't have his authority, his power, his Spirit, his heart, and his ear.

Although I knew I was justified by faith, I still thought that obedience was more or less up to me. I now began to discover that I could rely on God's promise that he was always with me and, by "faith working through love," do my work. During this time I dug deeper into my study of Galatians. I no longer asked, "How can I study this to help other people?" Instead, it was life and breath for *me*. I had to learn how to live the Christian life and be on the front lines with my husband without always collapsing. I also began to study the book of Romans, another book that for years I had avoided because I couldn't understand it. Now it too was a delight to read, study—and teach. I began a class on Romans for women from our church. I was only one step ahead of them as we gathered around our big dining room table, but our hearts were awakened to joy as we realized the truth of Romans 8—that because of Christ, God could never be angry with us again. All his wrath was poured out on Jesus; there is nothing left for his children. Though he may prune us as branches to bear more fruit (John 15), he never does so in anger or to punish us; it is always in love and only to make us more fruitful.

The ways God was blessing me were wonderful. I could never have anticipated what he would teach me next. Jack and I had been going to Uganda twice a year since 1979. But the challenges of ministry in that war-scarred country began to wear on me again. In December 1982, driving to Kenya in our old Land Rover, I said to Jack, "This is it! I'm never coming back to this country. This 'team ministry' is over." God gave Jack the grace to be quiet and just say, "Well, I'll have to go alone for shorter periods of time." And in June 1983, Jack, our son-in-law Bob, and another young man returned for a month together. On the day before their scheduled return, the telephone rang. Bob was on the line. He said, "Dad has had a heart attack." It did not take me long to decide what to do. "Tell Jack I'm coming out," I said. But before I went, I said, "God, you know how I feel about this country. Please go with me." And in the quiet of my heart the promise came very sure: "My Presence will go with you, and I will give you rest" (Exodus 33:14 NIV).

The next day I was on my way, not knowing what I would find when I got there. I knew what the hospitals were like; I had been in them. I knew the scarcity of medical care, but this time I *knew* that God was with me, and that his presence was far more real than the evil and the problems I would encounter. I can honestly say I went with joy. Our whole congregation and many others were praying. The church even sent a doctor, an old friend, to accompany me and care for Jack.

I now began to understand in a fuller way what it meant that I was not an orphan. I have the Spirit, I have the promises, and I have the Father's love. I have the sacrifice of Christ. My husband lived, and our ministry together became more effective than before and not so riddled with my confusions and unbelief. Perhaps Jack's perspective on our partnership at the time says it best:

> While I lay on a hospital bed in Uganda, Rose Marie's presence was like a light to fill the room. I am now up to about eighty percent of my workload, but it is a load Rose Marie shares with me.
>
> In her part of our ministry Rose Marie does counseling with women, but even more important to her is her Bible teaching. Her uniqueness is that she lays a sound theological foundation in justification by faith and sonship in all that she presents. She has a wealth of illustrations from her struggles and triumphs with people who have lived in our home and from the country of Uganda.
>
> But I think there is another basis for God giving us unity as we serve together. We pray together a great deal. We have a rule: "Never sit on a problem waiting for it to hatch a lot of worries." Stop and pray. We also have prayer meetings for the church in our home. I believe that prayer is, along with justification and adoption, the primary foundation for our ministry. Personally, I do not see how it is possible to have an effective ministry without the freedom given by justification through grace and the power given through prayer.
>
> What did I need to do before this team ministry was

possible? As a husband, I had to repent of my dominance and learn to listen to my wife—to show love in that way. I also had to teach her justification by faith and the meaning of our sonship through union with Christ. Once I repented, I expected her to be liberated with me. No way. So after a time, in desperation I gave her Luther on Galatians, and the change was amazing. I have seen some great changes in people, but Rose Marie's whole being was liberated by the truths that Luther taught.

LIFE CHANGES

The gospel also changed my expectations for us as a couple. I no longer expected Jack to be the Holy Spirit. *I* have the Holy Spirit. I know I am already "justified freely by God's grace." I did not constantly demand Jack's approval and sponge off his emotional life. I could give love to him as well as receive it. I didn't expect Jack to be perfect. If he made a mistake, I knew that his sins as well as mine were covered by the righteousness of Christ. I no longer expected to find wisdom or compassion in myself. It's all in Jesus, and he has enough for everyone I meet.

So deep is my sense that God accepts me just as I am that I can live unburdened by the expectations of others. As I talk to women in ministry from different parts of the country, they tell me about what others expect of them: to be the model wife and mother as they also minister in the church. I know that the expectations of others can be overwhelming. If I were to give you a list of practical tips on how to serve, it might only add to the pressure you feel. Instead I tell women that they don't have to be perfect because Another is perfect for them. They respond with such wonder and joy that I'm convinced that this is the overwhelming need today: *for everyone to hear the gospel—Christians and non-Christians alike.*

The gospel is the only anchor that will keep us in God's presence amid the stress of life. We all have longings for stability, approval, acceptance, security, and significance. Faith in Christ is what meets the true need beneath those longings and brings us to Jesus, enabling us to grow in grace. It is all we need. Jesus is enough.

2

Forgiveness

After my time in Switzerland, when I saw my heart as it really was and tasted the sweet grace of God's forgiveness, I asked Jack to forgive me for all my arrogant, selfish pride, my nagging, my presumption, and anything else I could think of that could have destroyed our marriage. He freely forgave.

But God showed me there was more that forgiveness could do in my life. He wanted to teach me a whole new way of living, a lifestyle of forgiveness and blessing instead of judgment and criticism.

I needed to forgive my mother for isolating our family from friends because of her paranoia, for rejecting and accusing my father, for pouring her sick energies into my mentally challenged sister and almost destroying her life, and for not being the nurturing mother I needed.

I also needed to forgive my daughter Barbara, who had rebelled against us and her Christian faith around this time, and

I had to forgive the friends who were such an evil influence in her life. I also needed to ask my children to forgive me. I especially needed to ask our three older children, Roseann, Ruth, and Paul, to forgive me for too much legalism in my relationship with them. I explained that I had been too concerned about their outward performance, always pushing them to conform and making their good behavior the goal of my parenting.

It was difficult for me to express to them the depth of my sin and the awesome grace of God's forgiveness—I was just starting to understand those truths myself. But I knew I had not brought them grace, and this is what I wanted to share with them, however haltingly. Jack's and my parenting style had not been particularly open and honest, so this was the start of something new. I'm not sure our children knew what to make of our first attempts to relate to them on a more personal level.

At this time Barbara was in the "far country" of rebellion, but one summer day she stopped by. Jack said, "Rose Marie, you need to tell her what God did in your life." Reluctantly, I did. We sat down in the cool shade of a big tree in our back garden. I told her that God had humbled me by bringing grace and forgiveness to my heart. My words were met with hostility and resentment. Humiliated, I backed off. It would be a few more years before Jesus revealed his forgiving love to Barbara. Then she was able to understand that she and I were much the same, both in need of God's grace and mercy.

FORGIVENESS AS A LIFESTYLE

When Jesus teaches us to pray, "Forgive us our sins, for we also forgive everyone who sins against us" (Luke 11:4 NIV), I did not realize that he meant this should go on every day—and sometimes many times during the day. God used the challenges that went along with ministry in Uganda to teach me these things. As Jack and I continued to make regular trips to that country, our son Paul said, "I think you two should go to Uganda full time." Until then I had been willing to make extended visits, but there was no way I was going to go full time! However, I was disturbed by my attitude and wondered why I wasn't as excited as Jack was to share God's love with Ugandans.

I went to one of our elders at New Life Church, David Powlison, and spent a long time telling him how hard life was in Uganda. After listening, he finally cut through all my complaining and said, "Rose Marie, do you need to forgive someone?"

The lights went on! Of course I did, and at that moment one particular Ugandan came to my mind. My real problem was that I was not cultivating a lifestyle of forgiveness. I sat before Dave and asked him to pray for me because I did not know how to do this. I had forgotten what the blood of Christ had done for me, cleansing me from all unrighteousness. I had forgotten the pit I had been pulled from, bringing me into the kingdom of the Son God loved. How could I *not* forgive? Yet I needed help. I said to Dave, "Please pray that God would bless me and give me the humility I need to forgive."

I went home and made a two-page list of every person and event that had bothered, upset, and embittered me in Uganda. I went through the list—it was long!—and asked God to forgive me for having such a bad attitude about it all. Then I asked him to help me forgive and bless those who were doing evil to one another. Then I asked God to forgive me for my attitude toward one particular person. I asked God to bless him and I continued to pray for him.

I shared what I was learning with others. One woman filled

up her page with a long list of hurts. She saw that she needed to forgive those who had disappointed her much more thoroughly than she had previously. She prayed and believed that Jesus had the power to help her, and she acted on it. She told me, "Once I had done this, I went to the kitchen sink, held a match to the list and burned it into ashes. Then I turned on the tap and washed the ashes away." Afterward she sought to forgive anyone who injured her right away. It became a new lifestyle. Jesus helped her to completely forgive a long list of people who had disappointed and wronged her. She also learned to pray for God's blessing on those who had hurt her.

What are we asking for when we ask God to bless someone? We are asking God's presence to draw near, to bestow favor on the person's life. Peter urges us to do this in his letter: "Do not repay evil with evil or insult with insult. but with blessing, because to this you were called" (1 Peter 3:9 NIV). The Ugandan man I had a hard time forgiving went seriously astray many times. But God remembered my prayer for him (and others' prayers, I'm sure). He has been restored by the Ugandan church and is laboring to bring people to Christ. As I wrestled with my unforgiving spirit toward this man, I found that forgiving the offender and asking God to bless him became a lifestyle for me. If you have been deeply sinned against, ask God to bring you to the place of blessing. It isn't easy, and may only come with pain and struggle, but like all God's commands, it is worth it.

PROBLEMS IN FORGIVENESS

It is especially hard to forgive when duty, order, and responsibility dominate. When duty supplants faith, I am blinded to the deep sins of my heart. In Switzerland, it took crashing down the mountain to open the eyes of my heart, but they can quickly close again if I move away from a simple devotion to Christ. Jesus reminds us in Matthew 7:5, "You hypocrite, first take the plank out of your own eye, and then you will see clearly to remove the speck from your brother's eye." When we do not forgive people, we hold their sin to be worse than our own. When we do not forgive, we do not experience God's forgiveness.

I received this letter from a friend.

My husband left me and my toddler son six months ago for another woman. Coping with his betrayal and deception has forced me to rely on Christ. I found that the deeper my needs, the deeper the reality of the cross. When my husband first left, I was overwhelmed. Everywhere I looked I saw filth. I looked in one direction and saw his lies. I looked in another direction and saw his infidelity. I turned my head yet another way and saw a cool and calculated malice. It was horrific and repulsive. I felt as if I was a spectator in a Roman forum, witnessing the bloodcurdling fight of two gladiators. I saw my husband and this woman fighting to their death through the sins of their lives. Although the scene made me wince with pain, I felt I was still a spectator.

Then I realized that I hated my husband with a rage that was frightening. It was all-consuming. I tried to convince myself that I only hated what he had done, but this was not the case. When I saw the poison of my hatred, the bloodied sword in my hand, I realized I wasn't a spectator in the forum at all. I was one of the gladiators in this sin-death struggle. There was no escape from this murderous fight in my own strength. I acknowledged to God the extent of my hatred for my husband and even confessed a lack of desire to change that emotion.

The life-giving power of the blood of Christ to cleanse was shown in my change of attitude. Christ's death had paid the price of my rage, producing a change in me. I could become a more godly woman by not hating someone who had wronged me. This experience gave me a few colors of the rainbow, bringing hope to me as I tried to recover from the wrongs done to me.

God enabled this woman to see that although she had not done what her husband had done, she had her own set of sins. This brought a release in her attitude toward her husband. It was a long struggle for her, but it no longer controlled her. She was free. Forgiveness does not excuse the abuse, but Jesus can give you a heart to forgive. You cannot trivialize what has been done to you, but by grace forgiveness is possible.

Forgiveness is forgetting in the sense that you let go of the offense so that you are not defined by the wrong done to you. I asked a pastor's wife who had been sexually abused as a young girl, "Is forgiving forgetting?" She said, "We still may have scars, but my goal now is to show God's glory. I no longer define myself by the wrong done to me. I place what happened in the nail-scarred hands. Jesus is the only one who will have scars in heaven."

Since Barbara's return to the Lord, I have shared a home with her, her husband and four children for more than twenty-five years. When I am in the States, I see her every day. It never occurs to me to remember her betrayal; I only marvel at what God has done and continues to do.

GOD'S COMMAND: FORGIVE AS CHRIST FORGIVES

"Be kind to one another, tenderhearted, forgiving one another, as God in Christ forgave you" (Ephesians 4:32). This is possible only as we remember the price Christ paid to make us right with God. Only then can we extend forgiveness. How deep is the forgiveness?

- "As far as the east is from the west, so far does he remove our transgressions from us" (Psalm 103:12).
- "Wash me, and I shall be whiter than snow" (Psalm 51:7).
- "You will cast all our sins into the depths of the sea" (Micah 7:19).

There are many more assurances in the Bible that remind us of God's total forgiveness, but God knows we cannot receive his forgiveness in our own strength. That is why he sent the Holy Spirit to live in our hearts. The Spirit opens our understanding to the depth of the Father's love for us and the power of the blood of Jesus, shed for our forgiveness. The Spirit is there to remind us that we are not orphans in an impersonal universe but sons and daughters of the living God. We especially need to remember this when we consider Jesus' command to forgive seventy times seven.

We know that God does not keep a record of wrongs, and we have the Holy Spirit to help us stop keeping our own records. My mother lived with us until she was 100 years old. There were many, many times when I had to forgive her—actually, more than seventy times seven! I was often very angry with her. She did things that caused chaos. She rarely listened and frequently went out in the ice and rain when we were not there to stop her. She was especially difficult to care for when Jack was diagnosed with cancer and had to go through chemotherapy. During that time, we needed to use one of the rooms in our home that was normally set aside for my mother and sister. My mother was angry and agitated that I had invaded her space, but we needed the room for Jack's care. We finally put her in a day care center, a place she did not want to be. One day she tried to climb out the window. When she was stopped, she tried to beat the caregiver with her cane. When she came home and I learned what she had done, she denied it at first. I said to her, "Mother, you cannot change yourself. Will you ask Jesus to change you?"

She put her head in her hands and said, "I am sorry. Jesus, change me." This was the first time I had ever heard her say she was sorry for anything. I struggled through the years with the "seventy times seven" equation, but it freed me from being controlled by her paranoia and gave me the freedom to not turn away from her but to continue to share Christ and even be thankful for her.

An early victory in that area came on January 27, 1950, the night before I was married. I wrote a letter of thanks to my mom and dad. In part it read, "Mother, thank you for rearing me the way you have, for encouraging me in my activities through grammar school and high school. Thank you for thinking that in many things no one could do as well as Rose Marie, for being proud when the American Legion Award was bestowed on me, for being glad when I was vice president of the student body of Jefferson High School. Thank you for providing an orderly and clean home, for great meals even during the Depression, for making do with little but seeing that Barbara [my sister] and I had new dresses for Easter and the first day of school. Thank you for the wonderful vacations in the redwoods. Thank you for loving the beauty of God's world and the music of opera." I am thankful that God gave me the grace to do that when I was young, and I am even more thankful that, over time, God enabled me to love my mother in the areas of her life that were more destructive. God can increase our faith's ability to express itself through love.

When my mother was dying, my son Paul asked her if she knew why Jesus had died. Did she believe he died for her? Her answer was yes. She died peacefully.

FORGIVENESS' POWER TO SET THE CONSCIENCE FREE

Jack and I once visited a family we had known in California. We had been told that the wife had been bedridden for two years with no obvious medical problems. Knowing that God could and would help, we asked if we could see her. Jack asked her some questions: "Do you hate anybody?" "No," she said. "Are you angry at anyone?" "No." "Do you resent anyone?" This time she said, "Yes, I resent my husband and my pastor."

Jack sent for the two men. She was able to talk through her resentments, her anger, and even her hate. As she laid it all before them, they asked her to forgive them—and she did. That night she had the best sleep in years and two weeks later she was back to work. That is the power of forgiveness—setting a prisoner free.

Another example of forgiveness freeing the conscience involved a young woman who tried to commit suicide by swimming out into the Atlantic Ocean. Some seminary students brought her to us. She was loaded down with guilt and expressed it in erratic behavior. Jack took her with him to one of his speaking engagements. His topic was "Jesus Christ gentles you." Later she told us that this was the first time she heard Jesus speak to her. She said to Jack, "Satan told me to kill you and your wife."

Immediately Jack said, "M——, I forgive you." She later said, "No one has ever loved me the way you and your wife have. I cannot believe I was trying to kill you." Years earlier she had made a pact with the Devil—a serious act that could have destroyed us all if God had not intervened.

I could tell many stories about the power of forgiveness, but they all pale in comparison to God's forgiveness of us.

Jesus had been up all night, beaten by the Romans, spit upon, crowned with thorns, and mocked by the Jews. Finally, he is nailed to the cross from which he cries: "Father, forgive them, for they know not what they do" (Luke 23:34). The only totally innocent man who ever lived becomes sin. He is wounded for my transgressions, crushed for my iniquities, oppressed, afflicted, and stricken, not for his sin, but for the sins of those who put him to death, for the sins of the world—for my sins. God was in Christ, reconciling the world to himself. God was setting in motion his grand plan of redemption. In Christ's death, the final price of our rebellion was paid. It is a mystery of love, "God forsaking God" for the sake of sinners.

This mystery of love continues after Jesus was raised from the dead and the disciples received the gift of the Spirit. At that time many priests "became obedient to the faith" (Acts 6:7). Perhaps they were the ones who had cried, "Crucify him."

There was someone else who understood the power of forgiveness. At this same time, God raised up Stephen, a follower of Jesus who was full of grace and power (Acts 6–7). He also was brought before the council for speaking words of blasphemy against Moses and God. Standing before the high priest, he reminded the council of God's story, beginning with Abraham and continuing on to the coming of Jesus, the Righteous One who would make Israel right with God.

Because he spoke the truth with wisdom and passion, he was stoned to death. Like Jesus he cried out, "Lord, do not hold this sin against them" (Acts 7:60). He knew what I need to remember daily: that Christ's forgiveness is total. Now, like Stephen, in the power of the Holy Spirit, I am able to forgive as Christ forgives. Unless the Holy Spirit continues to reveal more of God's forgiveness to my heart, I will dwell on an offense. I will harden my heart and refuse to bless the one who offended me.

Jesus drank the cup of God's wrath to the dregs. Now, when I drink from the cup at the Lord's Table, it is not God's anger I am drinking but God's blessing and forgiveness. I remember his body broken and his blood shed for me with a heart that has gone astray into the "far country" of pride and rebellion, too easily seduced from a "sincere and pure devotion to Christ" (2 Corinthians 11:3).

Through the years Jack and I saw how God worked his forgiveness in our family. We never again sat down with our children and said, "This is how it works." As God humbled us and taught us how to live from the perspective of grace, our children too were captured by Christ and his forgiving love.

I want to share one more story—a true story.

At sixteen, Esther, a gentle girl from Tanzania, was given as a bride to her wealthy eighty-five-year-old cousin. Thirty-seven cows were given to her father in exchange. Having been baptized as a child, Esther took seriously her desire to follow Jesus. The fact that neither her new husband nor his other wives were Christians was intimidating for her. The other wives were angry with her, and she often thought about running away. However, her family had spent the bride price to secure her brothers' marriages so she had to stay. She recounts, "After a time, I decided that I'd make the best of it and show that I could be a Christian even in this. Saying words means nothing if you don't have actions to go with it. So I started to show others the life of Christ, and they responded."

Though co-wives often live as enemies, Esther showed love, sharing what she had and serving not only her husband but also the other wives along with their many children. Her life, while never easy, has been sweetened by the family's response to the love of Christ. Her husband and three of her co-wives have become Christians. She also has great joy in the eight children born to her. Her influence even reached back to her own family where her mother and brothers put their trust in Jesus as well.

Esther is known as a woman of wisdom. She was the only woman sent to her church district meetings. Though she still has a gentle spirit, she is not afraid to speak up and inspires others to deal openly with issues that face the church in Tanzania.

At the time her story was told, her husband was 116 years old and Esther continued to serve her family and her community with the love of Christ.[1]

I was deeply moved by this woman who bent her will to God's will, accepted her circumstances, and brought forgiveness and blessing to her family and to all who read her story. This is the power of Christ. No one else can enable us to forgive, bless, and love in the middle of suffering.

3

Keeping a Good Conscience

A HEALTHY CONSCIENCE IS FREE TO LOVE

For many years my mother muttered, "I accuse you." She was deeply angry with my father because, without telling her, he had invested and lost money she had earned. She could not let it go, and bitterness settled in. Oddly though, her words of accusation were for herself, not for him. She couldn't forgive him and that, along with every other failure, troubled her conscience. She lived under a dark cloud of anger against my father and guilt for all that she hadn't done exactly right.

It was hard not be affected by my mother's words. I too had an accusing conscience: you failed in your duty; you displeased a friend; you were irresponsible. With these accusations a cloud of guilt would descend that I could not easily shake. I would struggle with deep discouragement and an uneasy sense that I needed to try harder to fix myself and others. In fact, I told Jack that he could put on my tombstone, "I Tried." I was kidding, but that was how I lived my life: trying hard to get it right but never succeeding.

In Switzerland, I experienced a strong sense of being forgiven and accepted by God. But I often struggled with the same things my mother struggled with—high standards of behavior for myself and others, a critical, unforgiving attitude toward those who failed to measure up (and that was everyone!), and guilt for my own failures.

Unexpectedly, God used something I really didn't want to do—public speaking with Jack—to teach me how to accept his forgiveness, forgive others, *and* have a healthy conscience that lived for God's approval instead of others'. Jack wanted me to go with him when he spoke at churches so that I could share with women what God had done in my life. But I didn't have a clue how to turn my experiences into talks!

At the first conference, my talks were a disaster, but since it seemed that God (through Jack!) was calling me to do this, I decided to study the book of Romans. As I studied, one truth became clear: God is righteous, and I have been made right with God because of Christ's sacrifice on the cross. Therefore, in a mysterious way I too am righteous. Though I barely understood it, that truth began to free my conscience. It also freed me to love others. So I started to share that with the women I spoke to.

The next conference took us to the Deep South. I was comfortable talking about the women of the Bible, so I started with Eve. After I spoke the first time, the pastor's wife invited me to lunch. We were sitting together in her sunny kitchen when she came right to the point. "I am a very angry person. I am angry with my husband, my children, our church, even the dog, and I hate this house. What shall I do?"

With the words of Christ and his gift of righteousness in my mind, I said, "I really don't know very much, but I think you just submit yourself to Christ's righteousness and give up trying to build your own record or the record of other people's approval. He will make it all right for and with you." "Is that all?" she asked. I replied, "As far as I know, Christ's perfect righteousness and yielding to it is the answer." She got out of her chair, went down on her knees, and sobbed out all her hate and anger to God. She prayed, "I accept your righteousness." She stood up and hugged me with a big smile, tear-filled eyes shining with joy. The guilty burden of her life had been lifted. She welcomed her husband home, apologized for her anger and condemnation of him and said, "I accepted Christ's righteousness for my own." He was astonished. Her conscience liberated; she was free to love. Paul wrote to Timothy, "The aim of our charge is love that issues from a pure heart and a good conscience and a sincere faith" (1 Timothy 1:5). When the conscience is noisy and cluttered, there is no real freedom to love.

Good news spreads fast. The next day, a group of women from the church asked me to join them for lunch so I could tell them what I'd told the pastor's wife. It was a lovely restaurant, flowers, white tablecloths—the works. I said, "You need a righteousness that Christ bought for you. Take it, it is yours." They said, "Is that all?" "Yes, that is all." We bowed our heads and hearts between the dessert plates and coffee cups and asked God for the gift of his righteousness. Some of the women were changed right then and there by Christ. Almost immediately others in the church were influenced by those who were shifting their reliance from their own "good works" to Christ. I was as astonished as they.

This type of encounter had never happened to me before, and it never happened again. I was amazed at the simplicity of the gospel and at its profound effect on the lives and consciences of these women.

At the end of the week Jack talked about the Ten Commandments and how the gospel cancels out the demands of the law. He said, "The gospel enables us to serve God with obedient joy and freedom because the blood of Jesus cleanses the conscience from the condemnation that living under duty and obligation always brings."

His diagrams that week explained the difference between true guilt and false guilt and helped me to understand why my conscience shifted so quickly from Christ to my own faulty record. When we live out of a sense of duty and obligation or live for the approval of others, our conscience shifts and false guilt, fear, anxiety, and depression likely follow. Living to please God—repenting of the true guilt that comes when we put anything besides God at the center of our lives, trusting in the blood of Christ to cleanse the conscience of dead works, and relying on the power and presence of the Holy Spirit for the tasks of the day—is truly the liberated way to live.

CAUSES OF A GUILTY CONSCIENCE

One of the reasons we come to feel guilty is that we move away from the cross and a desire to please God and live instead for the approval of others. Families have rules, our culture has rules, and the church often has hidden agendas. Our society encourages us to be successful, but if we live by a success/failure model rather than under the authority of Christ, we wound our consciences. As I spoke at different churches, I met women at different stages in life, some young, some old, some stay-at-home moms, some who were working full time and trying to balance career and family. But all of them seemed to be entangled in a web of rules: how to dress, what to eat, how to look, how to balance career and family, how to have well-behaved children and an attractive home, how to be successful, how to be a good Christian, and much more. Like me, they all tended to live under their rules or the rules others had for them, instead of accepting the gift of Christ's work on the cross for them. Like me, they were most troubled when their failures were noticed by the people around them.

If unfinished tasks, obligations, duties, successes, or failures dominate the conscience, we will feel guilty. Rules and lists tell us what to do, not where the power comes from to live in freedom. Paul writes, "For am I now seeking the approval of man, or of God? Or am I trying to please man? If I were still trying to please man, I would not be a servant of Christ" (Galatians 1:10). Living for the approval of others was deeply embedded in my heart. It took many twists and turns in my life before I recognized how selfish and self-centered that kind of life is.

It was our third trip to Uganda. Bob Heppe and his wife, my daughter Keren, were there with one-year-old daughter Gillian. Another American believer, John Songster, and Aggray, a young Ugandan, were also living with us in a house on the outskirts of Kampala. Since the country was still recovering from the neglect and abuse of Amin and much of the infrastructure was not in place, there was no water piped into the house. Jerricans filled with water had to be brought to the house daily. This water was used for limited bathing, washing dishes, washing clothes, and eventually flushing the toilet.

It was not an easy time or place in which to live. Since we were there to help care for Gillian, we encouraged Bob and Keren to go to Nairobi for R & R. After they left, Aggray came to us and asked if we could help him pay back a loan. He was frightened because the man he owed was becoming mean and vicious. In his mind it was a very big loan; in American money it was twenty dollars. I made a bargain with him and said, "We will pay the loan if you help me clean the house." He agreed. With a limited water supply, cleaning the house and doing the laundry were not easy tasks. We cleaned and studied the Bible together and the week sped by. Bob and Keren returned to a relatively clean house.

I like to give orders, and I like to get things done. My problem was that I didn't know when to stop. I should have stopped telling Aggray what to do when Bob and Keren returned. On the Sunday morning after they returned, Keren came to me and said, "Bob said to stop treating Aggray like a house boy." When I heard those words I was stunned and filled with guilt—a guilt I did not know how to deal with. It didn't help that on the way to church that morning Jack said to me, "You are dripping with guilt." Well, yes, I was, but it did not stop the gulping sobs.

What had happened? The bottom line was that I wanted to please Bob and Keren. It was true that I had continued to treat Aggray as if he were an employee, not a member of the household. Later, I apologized to Bob and explained that wanting to please them had gone so deep that I could not separate it from doing what I did before God alone. It is still a mystery why I did not apologize to Aggray. After all it was he I had wronged. I think I was so overwhelmed with guilt and shame that I did not and could not go to him with a humble heart. Addictions go deep. Approval, perfectionism, and legalism are subtle snares. They seem to work, but we are left with a noisy conscience.

SATAN'S ACCUSATIONS

When the heart has shifted from a "sincere and pure devotion to Christ" (2 Corinthians 11:3), we are vulnerable to the accusations of the Evil One. "The accuser of our brothers has been thrown down, who accuses them day and night before our God" (Revelation 12:10). One of his chief accusations is to insinuate that God is not for you and that he is withholding something from you. This was how he deceived Eve. He has not changed his tactics. He is a deceiver, destroyer, and accuser who will beguile us with thoughts like these:

- God does not understand.
- You do not have to do what God says.
- God has withheld something from you.
- You have needs he has not met.
- His promises are too lofty.
- If this is the right thing to do, you should not have such a big struggle.

Satan will always insinuate that God will not keep his promises to us. Because I grew up with my mother's words, "I accuse you" ringing in my ears, I was particularly vulnerable to having an accusing conscience as well. One day I said to Jack, "I believe some of this came from my mother." He prayed for me, and I was able to reject the accusations. But it remains a constant struggle for me. When I notice my failures, I always have to go back to the blood of Christ shed for me and hear his pronouncement of forgiveness, "The blood of Jesus his Son cleanses us from all sin. If we say we have no sin, we deceive ourselves, and the truth is not in us. If we confess our sins, he is faithful and just to forgive us our sins and to cleanse us from all unrighteousness" (1 John 1:7–9).

Rick Gray, one of our first missionaries to Bundibugyo, a remote area of Uganda, wrote,

> I hear the accusing, dark, and destructive suggestions of the Evil One:
> - "You are too busy to pray."
> - "You will probably fail in ministry to Ugandans."
> - "Your heart will never change, and neither will the hearts of the people in Bundibugyo."
>
> But there is another, much softer voice that I hear far too little. He longs for me to take to heart his words:
> - "You really only need to do one thing—stay close to me."
> - "Your worth depends on my blood that bought you, never on what you do."
> - "The ministry in Uganda is about me, and its effectiveness depends on me, not you."
> - "I am changing your heart as my beloved son, and I am also changing the hearts of my dear children in Bundibugyo."
>
> Perhaps what I need to do is not to adjust the volume control but to change the station I listen to! It seems like I've been stuck on a frequency blaring the same old deceit over and over again. I've listened to this trashy station for so long, I've forgotten that I have a choice. I can move the dial! Instead of listening to a cacophony of anxiety, contempt and despair, I can listen to the voice of love, peace, hope, and joy.
>
> As I contemplate a new term of ministry in Uganda, I realize that my friends in Bundibugyo also hear voices:

- "God is far off and does not care about you."
- "If you take those amulets off your baby, the child will die, unprotected from the evil spirits."
- "Only the witchdoctor can give you the power you need."
- "If only you had more money, then you would be happy."
- "All the important men have more than one wife."
- "Your life can never change."[1]

Rick realized that God's true, affirming, life-giving voice is much stronger and more powerful than all the opposing, lying, death-dealing voices. When my heart is not quiet before God, I have to ask where I have been beguiled. What lies am I listening to?

How do we stop listening to lies? How do we "change the station"? Satan will always cause us to doubt God's love and promises. I listen to men and women whose children have gone astray. Their chief doubt is whether God will bring them back.

MAINTAINING A GOOD CONSCIENCE

When Jesus told his disciples he was going to leave them, he also promised he would not leave them alone. He would send a helper—the Spirit of God—who would teach them all things and bring to their remembrance all the truth he had given them. He is the true Spirit of sonship, the Spirit who cries out in us, Abba Father. One of our major problems is forgetting how dependent we are on the Spirit of God for everything we need to live in a broken world, a world ruled by the Evil One. There needs to be a daily yielding to the Spirit to teach, to open the Word to my heart, to bring me into a deeper understanding of the cross.

Many times when I "felt" guilty, I didn't know what the real problem was. My feelings told me that something was wrong but not what it was. I was used to doing my own thing or listening to the lies of the Evil One, so I had to learn to discern the difference between the Spirit's conviction and Satan's lies. The Spirit discerns the thoughts and intents of the heart. He penetrates through excuses, defenses, blame shifting, proud independence, and love of approval. His conviction goes deep, bringing the real sins to light and reminding me again of the blood of Jesus, which was shed that I might be clean.

Richard Lovelace wrote: "We should make a deliberate effort at the outset of every day to recognize the person of the Holy Spirit, to move into the light concerning his presence in our consciousness and to open up our minds and to share all our thoughts and plans as we gaze by faith into the face of God. . . . We should look to him as teacher, guide, and sanctifier, giver of assurance concerning our sonship and standing before God, helper in prayer, and as the one who directs and empowers witness."[2]

There is always real guilt. We have not loved God with all our heart, soul, mind, and strength. We have not loved our neighbor as ourselves. We have not sought out the nations. This is why Christ shed his blood, so we could be free from condemnation, free from the curse, free to love God. That is why he has given us his Spirit to propel us away from our self-centered lives to a world that needs to hear the message of mercy, grace, and forgiveness. We never outgrow our need for the Spirit to lead us to Jesus, to the cross, to the blood, and to a deeper trust in the Father's steadfast love that endures forever.

Facing Loss,
Finding Life

Narrow is the mansion of my soul; enlarge it, that you may enter in. It is ruinous; repair it. It has that within which must offend your eyes; I confess and know it. But who shall cleanse it? Or to whom should I cry, save to you? Lord, cleanse me from my secret faults and spare your servant from the power of the enemy.

St. Augustine, *Confessions*[1]

One winter day in London in 1995, I read Augustine's prayer, looked hard at my soul, and saw how much work still needed to be done. So I prayed that God would enlarge and repair my heart.

Like most answers to prayer, God's response came in an unexpected form. At the time, my husband, Jack, and I spent each year in a whirlwind of travel and ministry. Even though Jack was sixty-seven and had some health problems, he was still directing

World Harvest Mission (WHM)—the mission he helped start; assisting our son-in-law Bob and daughter Keren in starting a church in London for South Asians; and working on his latest book. To accomplish all this we split our time between three countries—the United States, England, and Spain.

Jack loved all this activity, but it had its challenges for me as someone who always wanted life to be predictable, orderly, and safe. But as I spent my life teaching others that we need God's mercy and help every day, I was once again seeing how true that was for me. I prayed Augustine's prayer because I knew my heart had to be enlarged to accept our constantly changing schedule and to love a broken world more than my own comfort. As I prayed, I expected God to quietly deal with my heart, just as he had so many times before. Little did I know the changes that were in store for me as God answered my prayer for a bigger heart.

4

Death Disrupts

In January 1996, a few weeks after I prayed Augustine's prayer, Jack and I were on a plane, flying to Malaga, Spain. We planned to be there for three months while Jack wrote a book on suffering. As I looked out the airplane window, the sun seemed to take too long to slip over the horizon. I was restless, wondering why it moved so slowly. Then I saw the last amber rays sweep over the tops of the clouds. The beauty of the sunlit clouds was in contrast to the darkness I felt. I was tired of living out of a suitcase. I was tired of traveling. I was tired of never feeling like I was home. As we flew, I pleaded with God to let me stay in one place for a longer period of time.

We arrived in Spain and settled into our cozy apartment across from the Mediterranean. It had two bedrooms and a sitting room with a kitchen on one end and a sunny enclosed porch on the other. There we read, talked, and prayed. Every morning we bought fresh rolls and breakfasted on our patio in the warm sun.

Our front door opened out to a pool area surrounded by grass, palm trees, and bougainvilleas with red, purple, and orange flowers that crept up the walls of the community. Inside, even in hot weather, we were comfortable.

Jack worked on his book, but there was still time for long walks on the beach. We loved the beauty of the changing sky and the colors of the water. Life was peaceful and I forgot my conflicting prayers for a bigger heart *and* a settled life.

But soon our life became unsettled again, this time by Jack's health. He started having chest pains whenever he exercised. He loved to walk, but now he could barely make it to the beach. The pain was frequent and sometimes so severe that he had to spend the night in a nearby clinic. The doctors ordered an angioplasty, which revealed two blocked arteries. He was not well enough to travel back to the United States, so open-heart bypass surgery was scheduled at a hospital in Malaga. One of the best cardiologists in Malaga province would perform the surgery.

I can't remember what Jack and I talked about in the weeks leading up to the surgery, but I know we did not talk about his dying. In my mind, I was already mapping out the future. Jack would have surgery; I could care for him through recovery and maybe even hire a nurse to help me. This way we could stay longer in Spain, something I wanted to do anyway.

The week before Jack's surgery, WHM team leaders flew in to meet with him. We had a great time together, and many of them told stories about family members who lived long, productive lives after open-heart surgery. We were all optimistic. Jack had already survived a major heart attack in 1983, cancer in 1987, and a stroke just the year before. We were used to praying for Jack's health and watching God heal him against all odds. We expected no less this time.

The surgery took place on a Monday morning the week before Easter. The doctors had consulted with Jack's cardiologist in the United States, and they believed his heart was strong enough to survive the operation. But after surgery it became apparent that Jack's heart was failing. A few days after the surgery, when it was time to remove the ventilator, it became evident that Jack could not get along without it. Two of our daughters, Keren and Barbara, were with us, and Barb especially insisted on a heart pump for him. The last words he whispered to us were, "I love you."

When we were allowed to be with Jack in the ICU, we prayed, sang songs, and told him we loved him. One song we sang again and again was:

> O let the Son of God enfold you
> With his Spirit and his love,
> Let him fill your heart
> And satisfy your soul.
> O let him have the things
> That hold you
> And his Spirit like a dove
> Will descend upon your life
> And make you whole.[1]

We needed the song for our sake as much as for Jack's. We were holding onto Jack's life, and I know he wanted to hold on too. We kept praying that he would live, but one night the surgeon came in and said, "I don't think Jack is going to make it through the night." I thought, "This can't be happening. What about all the people praying all over the world?" It didn't make sense. Why would God take a man who had such a passion for his glory and such a desire for the nations to hear that God has made a way for the world to be right with him?

We knew God had the power to heal Jack but his condition continued to worsen. The next morning, I was driving to the Malaga airport to pick up our son, Paul. By this time I knew Jack was dying. I was praying through the Lord's Prayer. I stopped on the words, "Thy kingdom come, Thy will be done" (Matthew 6:10 KJV). I sensed God speaking to my heart with this thought: "Rose Marie, are you willing to surrender Jack if this is my will?"

Through tears I said, "Yes." It was a costly yes. I greeted Paul at the airport and told him, "Dad is dying." Paul spent the night in the hospital with his father. The next morning, Jesus welcomed Jack into his presence. Jack was settled in his heavenly home. It was April 8, 1996, Easter Monday.

We wept together—Barbara, Keren, Paul, and I in Spain, our other daughters Roseann and Ruth in the United States, our grandchildren and spiritual children and grandchildren all over the world. We cried for the loss of a husband, father, and grandfather. I was in shock. I busied myself with the arrangements to fly his body home. Duties and taxes had to be paid. I had to revise my Spanish will and close up the apartment with my children's help. I still remember the day Paul was cleaning the apartment. I sat outside in the warm sun, too tired to help, too tired to think—just too tired.

Once more I got on a plane, but this time without Jack. I traveled home alone to plan his funeral. At home, I was caught up in the details of Jack's memorial service. Although it was a hard time, I was surrounded by family and friends. Every day there were flowers, cards, and phone calls from those who loved Jack.

After the funeral I tried to settle back into life in the Philadelphia suburbs. I lived with Barbara, her husband Angelo, their four children, and my disabled sister, Barbara, in the large, old home that Jack and I had bought many years before. Barbara and Angelo had moved in with us eleven years earlier to free us to spend more time writing and doing mission work overseas. Now I was grateful that I didn't have to face life alone in an empty house. Still, Jack's death hadn't quite sunk in. I thought I would be more emotional, but instead I was numb. Jack's death and all it meant for me was just too overwhelming to face.

In the weeks following the funeral, I acted as if nothing had changed. One day I dragged Barbara out clothes shopping. Jack had often urged me to buy new clothes, but I always felt I could make do with what I had. I tried on clothes and remarked brightly to Barbara, "Your father would be so glad to see me shopping." She just looked at me. Later she said, "Mom, I thought you were losing your mind. I was so sad I could barely speak, and you were shopping!"

Two months after Jack's death, I attended the funeral of a three-month-old baby. As soon as I walked into the church and saw the coffin I started to sob, and I didn't stop crying for the next six months. I cried myself to sleep each night, listening to a song about a corn of wheat falling into the ground and dying. The song ended by saying the seed must die or it would remain a single seed. I know this refers to Christ, but it is also true of his follow-ers, of me. I was dying, and I didn't want to die, but even then I knew I did not want to remain a single seed. So I prayed, "Lord, this is me. I am dying without Jack. Please renew hope in me."

Death disrupts. Together Jack and I brought up five chil-dren; fed and housed troubled people; started New Life Church, watching it grow and plant daughter churches; and ministered in Ireland, Uganda, Russia, England, and Spain. We did everything together. When Jack was pastor and later mission director, I knew where I fit. I knew who I was. Now I felt like I had been sliced down the middle. The part that remained was lonely and fearful. I had lost a friend, a lover, and a partner. I missed the focus and direction Jack gave me and his emphasis on living out of the gospel. I missed his constant reminders to repent every day, to believe in God's love and power, and to pray constantly.

Without Jack I didn't know what to do. And I really didn't feel like doing anything. Getting out of bed every morning was a huge effort. I felt like my life was over, but I didn't think it was going to end any time soon. My mother lived to be 104 and when Jack died, I was 71 and healthy. I said to Barbara, "My biggest fear is that I am going to live for another thirty-three years." I don't think she had any idea of what to say.

Even though I felt like my whole life had been stripped away from me, I still had my lifelong habits of prayer and Bible reading. When Jack died, I was reading the book of Jeremiah. I kept reading and praying, asking God to give me direction and hope. I was desperate to hear God say something—anything—that would give me hope and help.

One day I came to the section where Jeremiah instructed the exiles in Babylon about what they were to do under the rule of Nebuchadnezzar. When I read the word "exile," it was as if neon lights were switched on the billboard of my life. Finally I had a word to describe how I felt—in exile. I sympathized with those who were thrown out of their home country to live in a foreign land. I felt that God had done the same with me.

The instructions Jeremiah gave to the exiles were simple. Even though they were banished from their own country, they were to continue doing everything they had done before. They were to build houses, plant gardens, marry, and have children. Since I too was an exile, I took these instructions for my own. I decided to continue what I had been doing before Jack's death. But for me this didn't mean building a house or having children; it meant continuing to tell how God humbled my heart to live out of a grace relationship with Jesus.

The first few times I spoke, I could hardly get through my talk without crying. A pastor friend called and prayed for me almost every day, and there were many others who supported me in a similar way. I knew I couldn't make it without people praying for me. The only thing that remained the same about my life was the wonderful story of God's grace to me, showing me my sins and giving himself for me on the cross. In every other way I was incredibly weak and needy.

It was good to know what God wanted me to do, but this did not deal with the haunting loneliness that no ministry, person, or activity could satisfy. Who was going to be my life partner? As I read through Isaiah, I came across this verse: "Remember no more the reproach of your widowhood. For your Maker is your husband—the LORD Almighty is his name—the Holy One of Israel is your Redeemer" (Isaiah 54:4–5 NIV). Apparently God was to be my new life partner.

Now I had to learn to live in the foreign land of widowhood with a new Senior Partner. I knew many South Asian women whose marriages were arranged. Often they met their future husbands for the first time on their wedding day. I felt like my relationship to God was that kind of arranged marriage. Like my friends who married without knowing their husbands, I did not know my new Husband very well. Does this mean I did not know God as my heavenly Father before this? No; God had worked powerfully in my life in the past. I had learned about grace in a way I had never thought possible: acceptance by God, forgiveness, no condemnation, a liberated conscience, the gift of being his daughter. But I had failed to cultivate that relationship. I knew God as a provider, a healer, one who loved the world and gave his Son for my sins, and a giver of grace but not so much as an intimate life partner. I had depended on Jack for that relationship. Jack was someone I could see, feel, touch, and hear for my strength and guidance. God knew this was not enough. He knew I needed to know him as my Husband, the one who was the Lord of Hosts, the ruler of nations, the God of all the earth. For me to know him in this way, I needed to be pushed out of my comfortable life (although it didn't feel comfortable at the time!). I needed all this if he was going to answer my half-hearted prayer for a larger heart.

God was gentle, taking me only one small step at a time. Understanding that he was my new Husband, I still had a story to tell of his mercy and grace. This was my first small step.

5

Living in Exile

Stooping very low engraves with care
His Name indelible upon our dust;
And from the ashes of our self-despair
Kindles a flame of love and humble trust.
He seeks no second site on which to build,
But on the old foundation, stone by stone,
Cementing sad experience with grace,
Fashions a stronger temple of His own.
Patricia St. John, *Patricia St. John Tells Her Own Story*[1]

Jack's death was the bulldozer God used to take my house—the life I had built around Jack—down to its foundations. I didn't realize how much my life revolved around my identity as Jack's wife until it was stripped away from me. As Jack's wife I was part of a team, a team that was sought out by many people. When Jack died, that all faded away. I was not part of a couple anymore. I felt alone at gatherings. I was no longer included in meetings at the mission. Being on my own felt strange and unpleasant.

At times I felt angry—angry that God had not healed Jack, angry at God's right to be God. I had spoken so often to women who were lonely, angry, distressed, and depressed, reminding them that they were not orphans, that God was a Father who truly loved them. Now I was the one acting like an orphan. Now I was the needy one.

All that was left was my foundation: the God I had depended on for so many years. I didn't know much—grief had left me confused and disoriented—but I knew enough to cry out to God for help. God used two simple things, prayer and his Word, to kindle a flame of love and humble trust in my broken heart.

LEANING ON MY GUIDE

I was like the man C. S. Lewis writes about in his book, *The Great Divorce,* who takes an excursion bus from hell to visit heaven. This was his experience when he stepped out of the bus: "Walking proved difficult. The grass, hard as diamonds to my unsubstantial feet, made me feel as if I was walking on wrinkled rock, and I suffered pains like those of the mermaid in Hans Andersen."[2] As a result, he had to lean heavily on his guide.

I too had to learn to lean hard. Every step I took felt sharp and unfamiliar. Going to social gatherings on my own, speaking on my own, writing to supporters on my own, going to bed alone—it was all unbelievably hard. But amid the pain came the certain knowledge that God was with me and that he loved me.

I learned to ask God throughout the day, at every lonely, sad moment, to be with me and assure me of his love and presence. And I was shameless in asking others to pray for me. Jack and I had learned to pray together, and I truly missed this. Gradually, in response to people's prayers, the self-absorption of grief began to break. I started noticing the needs of others and reaching out past the circle of my grief into their lives.

The first time I did this was with Carolyn, a friend I had met a year before Jack died. She and her husband (also named Jack) had both been widowed before they married each other. She understood what I was going through, and I often turned to her for prayer and comfort.

One day about three months after Jack's death, I called her and asked for prayer. She could tell how needy I was just by listening to me. Carolyn and Jack were doing major renovations in their home in Tennessee, so her Jack decided to send us both to Florida for a week's vacation.

While we were there, Carolyn shared with me that her life was ruled by duty, good manners, hospitality, and people's opinions. She lived her life trying to do "the right thing" and please everyone around her. When she failed, she was plunged into fear and despair.

As we talked, she told me that she was still struggling over something that happened when Jack and I had visited her the year before. During our visit, her stepdaughter went into labor with her first child. Carolyn was torn between pleasing us with a nice meal or going to the hospital to welcome her new grandchild. She went to the hospital, but she still struggled with whether she had done the right thing.

Carolyn admitted to me that what she was really worried about was her reputation and what we and her stepdaughter thought. I reminded her that the result of living for another's approval is always an unlimited burden of guilt and fear. As we discussed how our upbringings had impacted our lives, the cross of Christ took on a deeper meaning for both of us.

Carolyn saw that her love of looking good before people had bent her heart away from God. We remembered together that Jesus came because we are sinners, and it is only his death that makes us right with God. She took her love of reputation to Jesus, asked him for forgiveness for living for the approval of others, and believed again in the finished work of Christ. She no longer needed to live in the murky waters of others' approval and applause; she could live to please Christ alone.

SMALL STEPS FORWARD

After that week, I saw that even though I was physically and emotionally weak, I could still teach and mentor others. It was another small step of partnering with my new Husband. Leaning on my new Senior Partner, "I flattered myself my feet were already growing more solid. . . . I owed all this ease to the strong arm of the Teacher."[3]

Through the years the Spirit had taught me the power of the gospel to help Christians. This is where I felt comfortable. Many women who learn about sonship or read my book *From Fear to Freedom* ask the question, "What next?" My answer usually had been, "You need to study the Bible." This is always true, but now I say, "Take what you have learned, pray for divine appointments, and go to your neighbor." This is where I was to find true freedom and joy: in a heart for the lost, broken, and needy of this world.

Life didn't get any easier. My house was not rebuilt in a day, a month, or a year. But there was hope. I wasn't alone. God was with me, helping me to teach and mentor women again. But he had so much more in store for me than simply recreating the life I had with Jack. He was determined to enlarge my heart and my world, and, although I didn't know it at the time, he was going to take Jack and Carolyn right along with me. My life wasn't over, but neither was it going to be the same. Stone by stone, God was making me into a "stronger temple of his own."

6

Enlarging the Tent,
Enlarging the Heart

⌒

There was another big step I was to take in the strange land of exile. Jeremiah's counsel to the exiles in Babylon was to continue to do what they had been doing in their homeland. This I did: teaching, leading retreats, counseling women, getting my affairs in order.

The emphasis in my teaching was to help women walk in the freedom Christ purchased for us by his death on the cross. A great exchange had taken place at the cross: my unrighteousness—hostility to God, self-centered living, resistance to grace, rebellion, pride, and unbelief—was exchanged for Christ's perfect righteousness. I was now made right with God, free to love him and serve others because Christ died and rose again.

God knew we could never make it alone, so he sent the Spirit of his Son into our hearts "by whom we cry, 'Abba! Father!'"

(Romans 8:15). The problem, I would tell women, is that we act like orphans, living as if it were still up to us, living as if the Spirit never came and could never teach us or guide us in all the affairs of life. We go through the day believing that it is up to us to figure out how to solve our problems and get on with life. The result is that we live with an uneasy guilt and fear because we have not measured up to our standards or won the approval of others. For many years I had lived under a burden of unlimited obligations, duties, and responsibilities, and so my heart was easily condemned.

This still can happen when I am not trusting in the finished work of Christ. My conscience will always be uneasy and guilty when I shift my trust to myself and what I can do. As I spoke at retreats and conferences, I talked about freedom, using the stories of failures in my life. The Spirit opened the hearts of women to hear the music of the gospel. These truths strengthened my life too, but there was still something missing.

I continued to grieve the loss of my husband as a partner. I missed Jack's zeal for the gospel to empower his life; his passion for the lost; and his emphasis on prayer, humility, and repentance as a way of life. Missing all this often left me lonely and self-absorbed.

"YOU SHALL GO OUT IN JOY"

When I was not traveling, I attended my home church, New Life Presbyterian Church. One Sunday morning my son-in-law Angelo was preaching from Isaiah 58 about the fast God had chosen, a day "to loose the bonds of wickedness, ... to let the oppressed go free, and to break every yoke" (Isaiah 58:6). At one point Angelo said, "Speaking is not enough." I was startled. This is what I had been doing: speaking. What was the message? I opened my Bible to Isaiah 55 and read: "For you shall go out in joy and be led forth in peace; the mountains and the hills before you shall break forth into singing, and all the trees of the field shall clap their hands. Instead of the thorn shall come up the cypress; instead of the brier shall come up the myrtle; and it shall make a name for the LORD, an everlasting sign that shall not be cut off" (Isaiah 55:12–13).

I forgot everyone around me. The Spirit had reached my heart. God was going to send me out! This was the missing piece. To paraphrase Isaiah 54:2, he was going to enlarge the place of my tent—the curtains of my habitations would be stretched out. He was not only going to enlarge my tent, he would also enlarge my heart with his passion to reach the nations of the world, filled with people whose lives are thorns and briers. I knew the power of the gospel to free people to live as God's sons and daughters. But this was the next step, which I had often missed in my teaching: encouraging those who tasted freedom to share with the lost what Christ had done for them. Now God was calling me to bring that good news to the nations.

I went out of the service filled with joy. God was calling me to be a partner in making his name known. In the years ahead, I would see the oppressed go free, yokes of bondage broken, and God restoring people to himself and to one another.

THE CALL TO LONDON

The natural place to go was London, home to three hundred different ethnic groups. Jack had long felt that London was one of the greatest missionary opportunities in the history of the church.

He longed to see the gospel penetrate the Asian culture. As an answer to Jack's prayers, my daughter Keren, her husband Bob, and their children were already settled there, planting churches among the Asians.

I had my own history there too. I remembered in 1994, when Jack and I had marched with eighty thousand Christians through the streets of London, singing "Shine, Jesus, Shine." The group was composed of scores of new Christians, some just off drugs, some ex-prostitutes and former criminals. They carried a large red cross to show that Jesus was on the march with us. We ended in Hyde Park, praying for Christ to conquer the nations. We turned to face the north, south, east, and west and implored the Lord of the harvest to do his work. It was a great day.

On another occasion Jack and I brought a group of Americans to the community of Southall, London, where sixty-five thousand Asians live and work. Many emigrated with their families from India, Kenya, Uganda, Pakistan, Somalia, and other Third World countries. Walking through the crowded streets even today, you can see fruit and vegetable stands spilling out onto the sidewalks. Shops offer clothing, shoes, and jewelry that are all Indian designed and made. Bolts of colorful fabric are displayed for sale. The air is filled with Indian sweets and spicy kebabs, enticing us into the restaurants. The women wear colorful saris or Punjabi suits as they push strollers through the streets; Sikh men wear turbans.

Temples and other places of worship are scattered through the area. One of the largest Sikh *gurdwaras* (temple) outside India is in the center of Southall. There they revere an ancient book and worship gurus who lived three hundred years ago. Around the corner is a mosque where Muslims worship Allah and his prophet Mohammad. It is a strange, beautiful, exciting area. The nations are there.

Jack's purpose in bringing a group to this area had been to help us see that the fields are "ripe for harvest" (John 4:35 NIV). He wanted us to experience firsthand another culture that needed to know the good news of the kingdom. One of the places we visited was a small Hindu temple, where the devout came to placate multiple gods. The room was dark and the air thick with the fragrant smoke of burning incense. Statues of gods stood up front. Men and women came, bowed down, and left money and food at the idols' feet. Being there was a frightening experience for some on our team as they experienced firsthand the evil of idolatry.

After our visit, Jack gathered us in a circle outside the temple to pray against the idolatry we saw and against the idols of our own hearts. We also prayed against the lies and deceit of the Evil One. As we prayed, a few older, Asian women approached us and asked what we were doing. Jack invited them to join our circle, and he prayed that the light of the gospel would shine in their hearts. I saw that the Asians were open to prayer.

Another reason I felt confident in going to London was my experience with Asians in Uganda. When Jack and I were there in 1979, we stayed in a hotel with Hindus, Muslims, and returning Ugandan exiles. They became our friends as we endured the hardships of life together and prayed for God's help.

These experiences gave me confidence that God would be with me as I went to England.

OBSTACLES TO OVERCOME

Two things stood in the way of my going to London. The first was the continued care needed by my disabled, aging sister, Barbara. We all lived together and worked together to care for "Aunt"

Barbara. Although my daughter Barbara, her husband, Angelo, and their children were already taking care of Aunt Barbara, if I went to London, all of the responsibility for her care would be on their shoulders. But we talked it through, and both Barbara and Angelo urged me to go to London.

The second obstacle involved my speaking commitments at women's retreats and WHM events, including their conference, Sonship Week, which was an important part of the ministry. With Jack gone, there was a desire for me to stay involved in conferences like these. However, when I shared my desire to go to London with the mission leaders, they wanted to support me in this new call. Together we devised a schedule that would allow me to go to London and return to the United States for specific speaking engagements. The mission's cooperation removed the second major obstacle to my departure for London.

It was exciting to have a clear focus on what God wanted me to do: I would take Jesus' message to the people groups that God had sent to London. I was not able to go full time right away, but each year I spent more time there. The tent of my life was enlarging. The Spirit would use the fact that I am an older, gray-haired widow, often lonely and going in weakness, to reach into lives that were lonely, needy, and lost without Christ—just like mine.

7

Why London? Why Me?

⌒

When God called me to London, I was encouraged by events in my life that prepared me (somewhat) to reach out to Asians who had emigrated there. But on a heart level, I needed much more of the Spirit's work.

I knew that my heart had often been indifferent to the needs of the lost. That had been evident at the "Skis and Skeptics" evangelistic weekends. Choosing Agatha Christie over the needs of real people was pretty pathetic. I acted out of indifference, selfishness, and fear. *I did not have a broken heart for the lost.*

When Jack and I took troubled young people into our home, I thought it was manageable because they were under my authority. It worked well because I told them what to do and Jack gave them Christ and the message of the gospel. These folks were desperate. They believed the gospel and were changed. I did not realize that my heart was as needy as the hearts of the people who slept in our beds and ate at our table. My issue was self-centered control. *A heart centered on control has no room for brokenness.*

When we went to Uganda, it was an opportunity for God to begin to destroy the roots of my self-love. Self-love wants order, approval, and control. It wasn't long before I saw what evil had done to the people of that land. But I was troubled by my lack of love and my inability to cope with the evil I saw. *I did not have a broken heart for the suffering.*

Lilias Trotter, a young Englishwoman and gifted painter who gave up her career to become a missionary to the Muslims in Algeria, writes,

> It has been given to many to reap where others have sown, but if you want to sow and reap, then you must have a *broken heart* for sinners . . . and for us, in our small way, there is only one place where we can find the deepest heart-brokenness; it is down before the broken heart of Jesus, broken for our sins, for our selfishness, for the world about which we have cared so little. Emptiness, yieldedness, brokenness, these are the conditions of the Spirit's outflow. Such was the path taken by the Prince of Life to set us free.[1]

THE BLESSING OF BROKENNESS

The brokenness that God does not despise came to me in different ways. It was dramatic in Switzerland after my disastrous ski experience. And it was quiet when I sorrowed over my coldness of heart in Uganda, often with the realization that I did not believe Jesus' promise when he said, "I will never leave you nor forsake you" (Hebrews 13:5).

But there is another way I experienced brokenness. It was when my heart was broken by the loss of Jack. A year after he died, I woke up with these words intruding on my mind, "If only." I cried out from the depths of my heart, "Lord, if only you had not taken Jack, I would not be so incredibly lonely." My son-in-law Angelo said to me, "You have to watch that you don't fantasize the past or romanticize the future." He was right. It wasn't always easy being married to Jack, and it was a temptation to think that there was another man in the future who would take his place and care for me. At that moment, I closed the door to these illusions. But there was more to be learned about God's plans and ways.

HANNAH'S PRAYER AND GOD'S PLAN

The book of 1 Samuel talks about another woman with a broken heart, another woman who cried out to God, "If only." Her name was Hannah and her anguish was expressed in her prayer for a son. She was barren and lived for years being persecuted for it. Her pain was great, but what was not immediately apparent to her was that God was also in deep sorrow over his wayward people. They needed someone to lead them spiritually back to the Lord, and here God's plan and Hannah's prayer converge in a way that only God could orchestrate. I have thought a lot about Hannah, but a comment by Arthur Mathews sums up why God dealt with Hannah the way he did. In large part, it is the way he dealt with me. Mathews writes:

The hard thing for us to understand is the way the Bible emphasizes God as the responsible cause of all this trouble. Yet this is the point where we must stop until we begin to perceive the purpose of God in thus engineering things in Hannah's circumstances. What God did was to place on her heart a burden that corresponded to the very burden that is on His own heart. Thus God's problem is made Hannah's problem without her realizing it. The man-child that God needs in order that His word may come to all Israel is the man-child for which she is being so remorselessly driven to pour out her soul in prayer. Hannah's shut womb and its concomitant shame are God's means for hedging her into wits' end corner. There she will eventually lay hold on Him in desperation for the very man-child that He seeks and is waiting to give.[2]

Hannah became my lifelong friend. Through her, I learned that when God wants to move his kingdom forward, he puts his purposes and plans on the hearts of his people. When I knew Jack was dying and I prayed, "Thy kingdom come," his kingdom moving forward was on God's heart. It took years for me to embrace this truth, but the shift began when I was in London and saw Hindus, Sikhs, and Muslims embrace Jesus as their only hope to be made right with God.

Hannah endured years of suffering before she came to the place where, if God gave her a son, she would surrender him to God's purpose. Because of her heart's surrender to God, Samuel grew up to be a powerful leader who brought Israel back to God. He led God's people by becoming a man of prayer.

Then Hannah could sing a different song. She saw God as the first cause of life and death, poverty and wealth, humbling the proud and lifting up the needy from the ash heap. It takes a lifetime to learn all of what Hannah prayed concerning God's ways and will, but after meditating on her prayer I did come away knowing, "It is not by strength that one prevails" (1 Samuel 2:9 NIV).

A PARTNER IN GOD'S PLAN

Going in weakness, trusting in Christ, meant that I was to follow Christ into the hard places, whether at home or abroad. I was to be salt and light in a world that is decaying and in darkness, a world held in bondage to the "god of this world" (2 Corinthians 4:4). Partnership with the Father means I am in step with his passion to reach the lost, prepare a bride for his Son, and bring us through suffering to our eternal home. Through the years I have heard people say, "Some go, some give, and some pray." But we all need to pray, we all need to give, and we all need to go—even if it is just next door.

We live in a self-absorbed age. I need only look at my heart to know how easy it is to want life to be comfortable without stress, to be in charge, and to feel good about myself. It was always the bent of my heart to be safe, to protect my life, and to control people and circumstances. So why did God choose me to go to London? I believe it is simply because God delights in using the weak, the needy, the helpless, and, yes, even me, whose heart was not yet broken for the lost but heard the call to go.

Jack once wrote,

> What is expressed in Jesus' words [in the Great Commission] is really the commissioning of the whole new people of God. It is the emphatic demand of the Risen Lord placed on his people as a whole, and it has reference to the values, priorities, and programs of every member of every congregation. In a word, it means that we are all commissioned by the Lord in the Great Commission.[3]

I did go in weakness to London. Helplessness and weakness seem to have continued appeal to the Father's heart. In the years since, self-confidence, conceit, and self-sufficiency have been exposed and crushed many times. God continues to cement sad experience with grace. I have found that this is not only true for me but also for the Muslims, Sikhs, and Hindus I meet. As a team, we meet them riding in buses; sitting in parks; standing on street corners; buying clothes in our thrift store; visiting in their homes; at book tables with literature in their language; in their temples and mosques; on the school grounds; and at parties, weddings, celebrations, births, and deaths. We hear their stories, share their sorrows, bear their burdens, and invite them into our lives, our homes, and our fellowship. We watch as God makes them comfortable in our presence, feeling safe with us, and then embracing Christ as their only hope to be made right with God. Like Hannah, the cries of my heart were knit by God to his greater plan.

Learning to Pray

There is a profound mystery about the expansion of God's kingdom as it moves with power and authority into a dark and broken world. Then there is the wonder of how God uses the petitions, prayers, groans, and intercession of his people to accomplish his sovereign purpose of reconciling us, his enemies, to himself.

My husband and I had always prayed with each other and with our children, but I am not sure we understood what it meant to pray "Thy kingdom come." In a sense we were too busy building our own kingdom, which was mostly being sure our five children were well taught and properly behaved.

When our daughter Barbara rebelled against her family and her faith, we realized we were helpless to change her or ourselves. We were finally ready to pray.

O. Hallesby writes in his classic book on prayer, "Helplessness is the real secret and the impelling power of prayer. You should therefore rather try to thank God for the feeling of helplessness which he has given you."[1]

At the same time we were praying for our daughter, we were taking into our home people who had enormous needs. Our sense of helplessness increased. Jack knew we needed prayer on behalf of these folk because many comprised the core of our new church. We started an all-day prayer meeting every Tuesday in our home. People were encouraged to come and go as they were able and to pray for one another. Jack knew that prayerful unity releases us from our crippling personal anxieties.

The church also met in our home on Wednesday evenings for a potluck supper and prayer. One night there were seventy people, eager to hear the Word and to pray. A community was formed with the needy and broken who knew they needed prayer and a place where they were welcomed and understood.

Another way God taught us about our need for prayer began when Kefa Sempangi arrived at Westminster Theological Seminary as a refugee from Uganda. I have told about his coming to New Life Church and starting an all-night prayer meeting, pleading with God to depose dictator Idi Amin. Four years later, Amin was driven out and in December 1979, Jack and I took our first trip into Uganda at Kefa's request.

We prayed all through the day for everything. We were helpless in ourselves to save a country, to create jobs, to bring good government, to fill the stores with goods, or to help the orphans and widows. We did the only thing we could do and that was pray, and God heard. Lilias Trotter, the young missionary to Algeria during the late 1800s, wrote, "Each prayer-beat down here vibrates up to the very throne of God, and does its work through that throne on the principalities and powers around us.

We can never tell which will liberate the answer, but we can tell that each one will do its work."[2]

We began to see the fruit of those prayers for Uganda as people wanted to join us in the work and other churches became involved. Jack knew he could not manage the mission alone, so WHM was organized with a board of directors in 1983.

With every step, our confidence grew in the power God unleashes as we pray. In the early 1970s, Jack had been deeply impacted by John 7:37–38: "If anyone thirsts, let him come to me and drink. Whoever believes in me, as the Scripture has said, 'Out of his heart will flow rivers of living water.'" The unleashing of God's power in New Life Church and in Uganda was the result of trusting in the power and presence of the Holy Spirit, working through our prayers.

Jack wrote to one of our first missionaries to Uganda, "The beating heart of Christ's planting of churches is found in corporate prayer. It is through corporate intercession that the leader and the team of shepherds find release from fears, misconceptions, prejudices, pride, and self-will. The release comes as Christ himself visits them. He makes them one in heart and mind as they pray together."[3]

We had many needs. How were they going to be met? It was by asking, seeking, and knocking for the presence of the Spirit. The Spirit is the one who groans in us and presents our petitions to the Father in heaven.

In the same letter to that Ugandan missionary Jack wrote, "There is 'prayer' and there is God-given prayer. The former is superficial, the work of orphans who may be religious people but are unwilling to surrender human independence to the leadership of Christ. God-given prayer and praise have as their essence a waiting on God, a willingness to be wrought upon by the hammer and the fire of the Almighty, until the chains of self-centered desires fall away from the personality, and the love of Christ becomes the deepest hunger of the inner life."[4]

The lessons we learned during these years shaped our prayers for the rest of our lives. What follows are some meditations on prayer. I trust you will be encouraged to believe that the Spirit knows your heart as well as God's heart and his passion for a broken world. As you pray, you will find yourself in a mysterious way a partner in God's grand cause to redeem a runaway planet and to establish his kingdom on earth as it is in heaven.

8

Entering God's Presence
with Prayer: Luke 11:1–13

Recently I was standing in line in a bagel shop. A woman stopped and talked to the couple in front of me. I wasn't paying too much attention to their conversation until I heard the one lady say in an indignant voice, "I can't believe he said there is nothing left to do but pray!" Her tone indicated that she thought this was a cop-out, and of course there were things to be done. The couple she was talking to agreed.

Two weeks ago I was in a prayer group with some women. One said, "I don't understand why we need to pray when God has it all planned out anyway."

Perhaps you agree with one of these women or maybe you are somewhere in between. Hopefully you really want to learn to pray. You have a hunger to live in God's presence, and you want to make an impact in this sorry world. If so, I have good news for you. The parable in Luke 11:1–13 is all about how kingdom praying starts with helplessness. Our helplessness is one continuous appeal to the Father's heart.

PRAYER STARTS WITH HELPLESSNESS

"Now Jesus was praying in a certain place, and when he finished, one of his disciples said to him, 'Lord, teach us to pray, as John taught his disciples'" (Luke 11:1). It wasn't often that the disciples were humble enough to ask Jesus a serious question, but they had seen John the Baptist instruct his disciples, and they wanted similar instruction from Jesus. Ever gracious, Jesus answers their question by teaching them what we call the Lord's Prayer. He then follows with a parable, an earthly story with a heavenly meaning. At first, this story doesn't seem to have much connection to prayer or God's kingdom. But as we study it, we will find it has everything to do with prayer and living in God's presence.

The story starts with a midnight visitor. The man he comes to see has no bread to offer him. Middle Eastern hospitality demands that you serve food to a guest who comes to your home no matter when he arrives. Jesus says,

> Suppose one of you has a friend, and he goes to him at midnight and says, "Friend, lend me three loaves of bread, because a friend of mine on a journey has come to me, and I have nothing to set before him." Then the one inside answers, "Don't bother me. The door is already locked, and my children are with me in bed. I can't get up and give you anything." I tell you, though he will not get up and give him the bread because he is his friend, yet because of the man's boldness

he will get up and give him as much as he needs. So I say to you: Ask and it will be given to you; seek and you will find; knock and the door will be opened to you. For everyone who asks receives; he who seeks finds; and to him who knocks, the door will be opened. Which of you fathers, if your son asks for a fish, will give him a snake instead? Or if he asks for an egg, will give him a scorpion? If you then, though you are evil, know how to give good gifts to your children, how much more will your Father in heaven give the Holy Spirit to those who ask him! (Luke 11:5–13 NIV)

The man had a guest and nothing to serve him. So the first thing we learn about prayer is that it starts with helplessness. It is the essence of prayer.

I thought I knew how to pray. In answer to prayer, for many years God had provided clothes, housing, food, and education for our growing family on my husband's part-time salary while he finished his education. We prayed for God to provide, and he did. I felt safe in God's care. But when Jack became a pastor, his full-time salary no longer covered expenses. I lost confidence in God's sovereignty. I could no longer pray.

Praying starts with weakness—the acknowledgment that we don't know how to pray. But I had too much strength of a certain kind. I had strength to do my duty. I had strength to keep up an outward appearance of piety. This does not cultivate a heart that prays.

My love of control was so strong that I didn't know how to love or pray. Like the man in the parable, I was without bread. My problem was that I didn't know it. I also did not know where to get bread. I had to go through some very humbling experiences before I understood.

When we come into God's presence in prayer, we start by telling him we have no bread. We tell God day by day in what ways we feel helpless. In his book on prayer, O. Hallesby writes, "We should say to God as we mingle with our dear ones each day, 'God, give them each Thy blessing. They need it, because they live with me and I am very selfish and unwilling to sacrifice very much for them.'"[1] Every day we need to remember our inability to love God and others. Then we are driven to prayer, driven to knock at the door of him who has everything we need.

PRAYER IS PERSISTENT

The man's request for bread is refused in verses 7 and 8: "The one inside answers, 'Don't bother me. The door is already locked, and my children are with me in bed. I can't get up and give you anything.'" But Jesus says, "I tell you, though he will not get up and give him the bread because he is his friend, yet because of the man's [shameless] boldness he will get up and give him as much as he needs" (Luke 11:7–8 NIV).

Only used this one time in Scripture, the word translated boldness "implies an element of impudent insistence rising to the point of shamelessness . . . if by shameless insistence a favor may be won, even from one unwilling and ungracious, still more surely will God answer the earnest prayer of His people. God's willingness to give exceeds our ability to ask. The parable teaches by way of contrast, not by parallel."[2]

So the second thing we learn about prayer is that it is persistent. Apparently the man without bread had nowhere else to turn. He knows his neighbor, and he knows he has bread. So he is going to keep on knocking until he gets what he needs. He will not be shamed before his guest. The heart of prayer is when we finally acknowledge our own helplessness: no bread means we have no human wisdom, strength, or resources to manage and control our lives. Then we go boldly and persistently to the One who is seated at the right hand of God for all the grace we need.

Ken Bailey is a man who read Jesus' parables to people in remote villages of Palestine and listened to their responses. He notes that the man who needs bread refuses to give up. He continues to knock boldly and persistently until finally the so-called friend gets up and gives him what he needs. By this time the whole village has probably been aroused by the continued knocking and loud dialogue between the two men. One man is shouting and knocking outside the door and the one inside is shouting his answers. Of course, now all the children are awake and will tell the story tomorrow to their friends. The man in the house will be shamed by the village if he doesn't give his neighbor bread, and the man with a hungry midnight visitor will be shamed if he has no bread to set before him. Bailey concludes, "I tell you . . . he will not give him anything . . . because of being his friend, but because of his avoidance of shame, he will get up and give him whatever he wants."[3]

Jesus then applies this parable in verses 9 and 10: "Ask and it will be given to you; seek and you will find; knock and the door will be opened to you. For everyone who ask receives; he who seeks finds; and to him who knocks, the door will be opened." The reward for persistence in prayer is that we will get the bread we need not only for ourselves but also for the friends at midnight—those in our lives who need what only Christ can give. Our persistence means we will not be shamed by a prayer life that has no vitality in it.

The words are better translated, "Keep on asking, keep on

seeking, keep on knocking." I was in Ireland years ago with my daughter Keren; her husband, Bob; and their daughters Gillian and Natalie. The two little girls and I would walk together to the store, and on our way back we passed a building where delicious smells of baking would hit us. There was no window, but there was a door. I said, "Let's knock on the door and see if they will sell us a loaf of fresh-baked bread." I knocked on the door, and no one answered. I knocked again, and no one answered. I knocked a third time. No answer. So we left. As we walked home, the thought came to me, "Rose Marie, this is how you pray. You ask one or two times and then you stop if the answer does not come."

Jesus then expands on the asking, seeking, and knocking: "Which of you fathers, if your son asks for a fish, will give him a snake instead? Or if he asks for an egg, will give him a scorpion? If you then, though you are evil, know how to give good gifts to your children, how much more will your Father in heaven give the Holy Spirit to those who ask him!" (vv. 11–13).

I understand what Jesus is saying because even though I am evil, I know how to give gifts to my children. In my travels I am always looking for gifts for my children, their spouses, and their children. That means a lot of presents for birthdays and Christmas every year. If I am always buying gifts, how much more will our Father give the Holy Spirit to us who ask?

THE GIFT OF THE SPIRIT

Living in God's presence is not only our privilege and delight, it also pleases God. As we ask for the Holy Spirit, God's response is to give us himself. He lives in our hearts, and thus, we are continually in his presence.

In his letter to the Ephesians, Paul prays that God would give them the Spirit of wisdom, that they might know Christ better. He prays that they may be strengthened "with power through his Spirit in your inner being, so that Christ may dwell in your hearts through faith, [so] that you, being rooted and established in love, may have power, together with all the saints, to grasp how wide and long and high and deep is the love of Christ, and to know this love that surpasses knowledge—that you might be filled . . . [with] all the fullness of God" (Ephesians 3:16–19 NIV). The Spirit is the one who gives us a deeper walk with Christ and helps us understand more fully the Father's love for us.

As you hear about the friend at midnight, you might be discouraged and think that prayer requires too much effort. There are too many distractions, too many pressures and problems, too much to do to have this kind of persistence in prayer. Be encouraged: the whole Trinity is involved in our prayer endeavors.

The book of Hebrews tells us that Jesus, our Great High Priest, is at the right hand of the Father, interceding for us. "We do not have a high priest who is unable to sympathize with our weaknesses, but we have one who has been tempted in every way, just as we are—yet was without sin. Let us then approach the throne of grace with confidence, so that we may receive mercy and find grace to help us in our time of need" (Hebrews 4:15–16 NIV). Hebrews 7:25 adds that "he always lives to intercede for [us]."

And Paul wrote in Romans 8:26–27, "The Spirit helps us in our weakness. We do not know what we ought to pray for, but the Spirit himself intercedes for us with groans that words cannot express. And he who searches our hearts knows the mind of the Spirit, because the Spirit intercedes for the saints in accordance with God's will" (NIV). You are in partnership with the Father who loves you, the Spirit who intercedes for you, and the Christ who died for you and intercedes for you at the Father's right hand. You can't lose! The Trinity is involving us in the rescue of a fallen planet as the Father prepares a bride for his Son. In a mysterious way God invites us to join in prayer to accomplish this work.

Looking again at Luke 11, Jesus says it is unthinkable that a father would give a snake or a scorpion to a son who asks for fish or bread. Snakes and scorpions are what Satan feeds us. He wants us to doubt God's love for us; he feeds us with fears about the future; he questions God's providence; he waters down the promises; he invites us to question God's goodness; and he entices us with thoughts that we can take charge and be in control. This is why we need the Spirit. We need his wisdom to discern the lies, stand against them, and hunger instead for Christ, to walk in his presence and to appropriate all he has for us.

HOW I LEARNED TO PRAY

God used two major events in my life to teach me how to pray. The first was learning to pray with authority for our daughter Barbara when she left the faith. As we got to really know who she was as a young adult, we saw clearly that, like the man in the parable, we had no bread, no resources to help her. If we could have helped her ourselves, we would have, but nothing seemed to penetrate the lies she believed. The Spirit showed us how to pray against Satan's lies and to rely on the authority of Christ over her life. We prayed that God would put a hedge about her, using the prayer of Hosea when his wife turned to other lovers. He writes, "Therefore I will hedge up her way with thorns, and I will build a wall against her, so that she cannot find her paths" (Hosea 2:6).

In our prayers, we battled against the kingdom of darkness that seemed to claim Barbara's life. We reminded Satan that he had no right to her life. We remembered God's covenant promise that he would be a God to us and to our children. We prayed against the obvious sins in her life. We asked the Father clearly and specifically to do what we asked for his glory. We did it in the context of praise for the sovereignty of Christ and submission to his will. We were relying not on a formula but on Christ's sacrifice and all that it accomplished. We had been praying for years, but now we were praying with confident faith that God had heard.

A few weeks after we started praying for her with authority, Barbara called and said, "I can't lie anymore . . . . I am also going to pay my taxes." Months later she left the drug scene and came back home. It would be another four years before Jesus in his love claimed her heart. But we were content to wait, to welcome, and to pray.

The second major event was our trip to Uganda in 1979. It was a country in ruins, filled with chaos, evil, and brokenness. Only Christ could bring life out of such darkness. We stayed in the only "safe" hotel under difficult conditions. Everywhere we turned, someone told a story of brutality that was almost too difficult to hear. We were in a country with no resources, but God gave us a ministry of prayer among those living in the hotel.

First, we prayed for safety since the country was still unsettled. We had a 7 p.m. to 7 a.m. curfew since there was a good chance we would be shot if we went outside. We prayed for water, which came only sporadically through the faucets. When it did, we filled the tub, because we never knew when it would come again. We prayed for decent food since the good food delivered to the hotel in the morning was usually stolen and we would be served leftovers in the evening.

The hotel was filled with Asians from India and Pakistan,

expatriates, returning Ugandans, and public officials setting up the new government. Jack started a Bible study with Ugandans and Muslims. It was usually noisy and full of tension. One day a woman who was part of the new government joined the group. She pled with us to pray right then because the government was threatening to go Communist. We prayed. Four hours later, she returned and said that our prayers had been answered.

We had been there about two weeks when we were awakened to hear that a prominent Muslim man from Pakistan had suffered a major heart attack at five o'clock that morning. The doctor would not break curfew to come, and the victim's face was gray. People were gathered in the hallway near his room. Jack gathered them in a circle and led in prayer for the man's healing. Then Jack and another man took him in a chair down the elevator to a taxi and to the hospital. There he was virtually untreated, so we went almost every day to pray for him. God healed him.

Then his friend came to Jack with inflamed, red eyes. He pled with Jack to pray for him. Many children in the hotel were sick, and often Jack was called on to pray for their healing—and they were healed. Jack always prayed in Jesus' name and reminded them that only Jesus could heal them.

We prayed with church leaders who met in our room for tea and teaching. The teaching was always followed by preaching in the open-air market where we did battle against the witch doctors who did their incantations at the other end of the square. We prayed for conversions and God added to his church. I recently heard that fifty churches have been planted out of the first "mother" church.

These people were without any resources to help themselves. Like the man in the parable, they were without bread. But we had learned where to get bread for our family, so we kept asking for the power and presence of the Spirit for the people in Uganda. We knew what it was like to be without bread in our relationship to Barbara, but we had learned to keep on asking, seeking, and knocking for the Spirit. Praying with authority for Barbara was the basis of the extraordinary answers to prayer we witnessed in Uganda. God had enlarged our hearts to pray for others as we learned to pray for our family. As *we* lived in God's presence, we brought *them* into God's presence through our prayers.

O. Hallesby writes, "The work of praying is prerequisite to all other work in the kingdom of God, for the simple reason that it is by prayer that we couple the powers of heaven to our helplessness, the powers which can turn water into wine and remove mountains in our own life and the lives of others, the powers which can awaken those who sleep in sin and raise up the dead, the powers which capture strongholds and make the impossible possible."[4]

This is what we pray for when we say, "Your kingdom come." Where is the Spirit leading us in our praying? We are praying that God's kingdom would rule over the affairs of nations, that his people would be salt and light in this dark world, and that Jesus would come quickly. To pray "Thy kingdom come" is sometimes hardest to pray because it means we have to stop our own kingdom building. If we are really, deep down honest, we are usually seeking our own kingdom. Our will, our way, our plans, our purposes, our desires are not necessarily what the Spirit desires for the growth of God's kingdom.

TEACHING PEOPLE TO PRAY

Jack and I learned to be partners together in prayer for God's kingdom to come. The parable of Luke 11 was our model, and the

Spirit continued to teach us. We began to see the value of having people share their needs with others not for advice but for prayer. Sometimes the hardest place to start is to admit that we have a need. Often we don't think to ask people to pray until we have run out of options.

My friend Marlene was a nurse manager at a local rehab hospital. State inspection was coming up, and she felt responsible for her unit and for the accreditation of the hospital. She knew that a lot of work had to be done, and she was full of fear that she and the hospital would fail. I encouraged her to write friends and ask them to pray for her. She sent out about twenty letters appealing for prayer.

After the inspection, she wrote to those who prayed:

> Thank you for your prayers for me, my staff and the hospital. God has answered them exceedingly above anything I could ask or think. Our hospital passed the inspection. On a personal level, God used the pressures of this situation to reveal to me once again how quickly my heart becomes dull, hard, fearful and anxious. Enveloped by a wall of unbelief, I felt abandoned. Friends, as you prayed, the wall of unbelief crumbled. I was reminded I have a Father who loves me unconditionally. As I repented of my sinful attitudes and looked to Jesus for forgiveness, I was overwhelmed with gratitude for Jesus' love and mercy. Also, I experienced a peace and a deeper trust in God's plan for my life. This has renewed my desire to share the love of Christ with others.

I shared this letter with her recently. She said, "Did I write that?" After reading her the letter, we walked in the mall together. God led us to share Christ with a bitter, elderly woman. This is what happens when God renews our hearts.

I came home from England to speak in St. Louis at a Sonship Week sponsored by WHM. I came with much weakness. Our lectures had been critiqued and I had been told that I didn't finish my sentences and didn't speak with enough passion. I had also been told not to read my talks because I lost freedom and spontaneity—but I was reading my talks to make sure I finished my sentences! In short, I knew I needed prayer.

I stayed with a friend in St. Louis. We spent a lot of time bringing her needs, my needs, family needs, and the needs of the people at the conference before the throne of grace. At the end of the week she said, "Rose Marie, three of us walked together this week. You have helped me to walk in the presence of God. Thank you. Now I want to do the same with other women."

When we humble ourselves before God and others, acknowledging our need, then when God answers, he is glorified and his kingdom moves with power into all our lives. We are invited to "come boldly unto the throne of grace" (Hebrews 4:16 KJV). Come believing that God's plan is good and that the Spirit has all the resources to enable you to live before him and to bring others into his presence.

Be people of love. Be people of faith. Be people of prayer. Do you long to be changed? To see people change? To be part of God's reclaiming the world for himself? Get in a prayer meeting. Go to the throne of grace and bring others with you. In the delays of your life, don't live in the land of "If only." Don't interpret the interruptions of your life as God turning from you. In your prayers, ask for the Holy Spirit—and expect God's kingdom to come.

9

Groaning and Glory: Romans 8

I know many things about prayer. I know the content of the Lord's Prayer. I have cried and prayed through many psalms. I have been in countless prayer meetings where I have been prayed for and have prayed for hurting people. In spite of all this, I have to say from my heart that I do not know how to pray. But I do know how to groan. That I'm good at!

Jesus himself was no stranger to groaning and weeping. There were times when he went to pray in solitude. Another time Jesus groaned as he cried out to his Father to let the cup pass from him. He was overwhelmed with sorrow to the point of death. He even wept over the people who would soon crucify him: "Would that you, even you, had known on this day the things that make for peace! But now they are hidden from your eyes. . . . You did not know the time of your visitation" (Luke 19:42, 44).

THE GROANINGS OF PRAYER

If groaning is part of praying, then I know a little about prayer. As Jack and I prayed for many different needs in many different circumstances, we saw the astonishing reality that our prayers matter, yet we knew very little about how to pray. We were weak. We not only knew this from experience, we were taught this as we studied Romans 8:26–27 and the part the Holy Spirit has in our praying. It reads: "Likewise the Spirit helps us in our weakness. For we do not know what to pray for as we ought, but the Spirit himself intercedes for us with groanings too deep for words. And he who searches hearts knows what is the mind of the Spirit, because the Spirit intercedes for the saints according to the will of God."

In his book, *The Crown and the Fire*, N. T. Wright states:

> The Spirit sustains and supports us . . . in our weakness. . . . We look at the world and long to bring to it the justice and peace, the *Shalom*, for which it is yearning. And we don't know how to do it. . . . But at the very moment of this weakness . . . we have the assurance that the Spirit is doing the praying that we cannot do. God is sharing, by his Spirit, in the groaning of creation and the groaning of the church. . . . Prayer at the deepest level is here understood as God calling to God from within the created and groaning world . . . God the Spirit, dwelling in the hearts of [his] people as they dwell in the midst of the broken world and calling to God the Father . . . and being certainly heard.[1]

The whole creation is groaning to be delivered from the bondage of decay. We ourselves groan as we wait for our adoption as sons, and the Spirit groans, presenting our petitions to the Father.

And the Father listens and is preparing his answer, which we read in Romans 8:28: "We know that for those who love God all things work together for good, for those who are called according to his purpose." Your groanings of fear, strained relationships, unfulfilled expectations, sickness, disappointments, loneliness, failures, guilt, and abuse may hinder you from believing that God works all things for your good. But do not define yourself as the orphan who is left alone. I believe the Spirit groans for us, that we might fully enter into the delight of being sons and daughters of the living God. And the Spirit also groans for a fallen world.

Sometimes our prayers to God can only find expression in groaning. This needn't discourage us. O. Hallesby, in his famous book on prayer, writes: "My helpless friend, your helplessness is the most powerful plea which rises up to the tender father-heart of God. He has heard your prayer from the very first moment that you honestly cried to him in your need, and night and day he inclines his ear toward earth in order to ascertain if any of the helpless children of men are turning to him in their distress."[2]

THE POWER OF THE SPIRIT

The truth of my helplessness and my urgent need for the power and presence of the Spirit is something I encounter constantly in ministry. I'm a member of a team that lives and works among Asians—mostly Sikhs, Hindus, and Muslims. Members of these Asian communities are knit tightly together by family, religion, duty, obligation, responsibility, food, dress, and tradition. But when we get to know these people, we find just below the surface deep anxieties, guilt, shame, anger, rebellion, fear, black magic, and demons.

These realities were brought home to me vividly one evening when about fifteen Punjabi women gathered in my friend
Balvinder's home for dinner and a time of getting acquainted.
Balvinder has been a vital part of our community since she followed her father to church and eventually embraced Jesus for herself. She is a widow with three children from a Sikh background.
She works in our charity chop and befriends many of the older
ladies who speak very little English. She serves them tea, prays for
them, helps them listen to tapes in Punjabi, and often takes them
into her home. These women were Balvinder's guests that night.
She was eager for them to know that Jesus was the only one who
could meet their need.

After the meal we gathered in her living room. As the women
began to feel comfortable with one another, they started trading
stories about black magic. Each one was convinced that what she
had heard and seen was true. I sat there appalled, and in my heart
I cried out for the Spirit to show me how to break into the discus-
sion. The Spirit brought to my mind the incident where Christ's
power healed the man who was possessed by a legion of demons.

By now all the women were talking—how could I break in? So
I prayed for even a slight pause. It came and I took advantage of it
and said, "Ladies, there is one who can break the power of black
magic and demons, and that is Jesus." I went on to tell the story
and after that there was no more talk of demons. But later that
night, around midnight, one of the women telephoned Balvinder
and cried for help because her daughter and niece were possessed
by demons.

A group of us went to the home of the two women while others stayed home and prayed against demon oppression. This was
a demonstration of the power and presence of the Spirit and also
of a community of believers uniting in Spirit-filled prayer against

the kingdom of darkness. Eventually my daughter and son-in-law took the daughter into their home, and the folks at our church, Masih Ghar, embraced her also.

In the face of such spiritual realities, the fact that the Spirit is groaning over us as we pray is an unbelievable comfort. The Spirit, who searches our hearts, knows what is going on, so we don't need to come with prayer formulas or just the right words. God sustains and supports us in our weakness and answers our prayers according to his will, for his glory. The Spirit prays with us and for us as we groan over our weaknesses and sins, and over a world, which we often care so little about, that is desperate to know the peace that only a right relationship with God can give.

How does that work in a practical way? On our team, we pray that God will work in the hearts of people and we often pray for their dreams.

FARIAH

We met Fariah at a Gujarati dance called Garba. She is from a Muslim background, the kind of community I described earlier. She had been in an abusive marriage and now lived with her mother. She was brought up believing in the Koran and was faithful in her prayers.

Several years ago, a friend invited her to church. She was moved by the worship and truly felt loved. The simple songs and prayers so affected her that she couldn't stop crying. She had been praying five times a day at the mosque and had never felt this way.

Someone sitting behind her saw her crying, and when the pastor gave the invitation to come forward, the woman said, "Come, I will go with you." Fariah went, but when they handed her a leaflet to fill out, she became angry and accused them saying, "You are trying to convert me!" and she left. She went back to the mosque and started praying harder but eventually decided to return to the church because of the worship—but only for the worship. This went on for two years.

During this time she had a dream that frightened her. She felt lifted out of her bed and shaken from side to side. In her dream she called to Allah, but nothing happened. During this time she started to seek help from tarot cards and actually felt demons enter her. Terrified she went to the pastor of the church where she enjoyed the worship and told him her story. He prayed for her, and the demons left. After that she started going to church, but this time she was truly searching for the truth. She picked up a leaflet left at another church about a meeting of believers in Harrow. She went and there met a teammate of mine. Later I met the two of them for coffee and shared the gospel with her. Soon after, she came to our house and met a Muslim convert who helped her and prayed for her.

Then in another dream she was in a crowded room that was rapidly filling with mud. She felt someone lift her out of the mud—someone she knew to be Jesus. After talking to a friend, she finally understood the meaning of Jesus' sacrifice. There were many people that the Spirit used to draw her to himself.

Fariah continued to slip in and out of my life, but recently she called in distress and asked if she could meet with me to study the Bible. My son-in-law Bob said I should give her solid teaching about the Holy Spirit because there is a lot of confusion about the baptism of the Spirit. This was wise advice, and it is what I began to do. She had been feeling guilty because she had not told her mother that she was a Christian. So the Spirit's work in her life continues.

Here again we see the work of the Spirit wooing Fariah in the midst of a community of believers involved in her life. We pray, drink coffee, telephone, share dinners and serious discussions, and answer her questions graciously and honestly. We are convinced that God is working through us in our weakness, always supporting and always sustaining.

WEAKNESS AND FAITH

Jack and I learned through the years how dependent we were on the Spirit, not only to present our groanings to God, but to teach us his ways through the crises in our lives. He used them to build our faith in the God who answers the groanings and yearnings of our hearts. You will soon be praying through streets where thousands of Asians live. Jesus tells us to pray, "Father, hallowed be your name. Your kingdom come" (Luke 11:2). We need the Spirit to teach us how to pray because we are usually more concerned with building our own kingdoms than God's kingdom—the one where he receives all the glory. How many of us secretly want our names to be hallowed rather than God's? We daily need forgiveness and we daily need to forgive others. Each day we are tempted to live for ourselves, our glory, our praise—and not the praise that comes from God. Knowing this about ourselves, all through each day we need to ask for the Spirit, for the presence of Christ in our lives to pray as Jesus taught his disciples to pray.

It is no accident that fifty-two Americans are here in Southall, the home of more than 150,000 Asians, to walk the streets and pray. God is a missionary God. His plan is to rescue a rebellious world by bringing his people out of darkness into his marvelous light. His plan includes our cooperation and our prayers. In a mysterious way, God orchestrates the events of our lives, bringing us to the place of brokenness and humility to teach us how to pray. Then he involves us in his desire to reach the nations. The Holy Spirit continues the living presence of God in our lives. He guides us into all truth and equips us to carry on the ministry of Christ.

A year before he died, my husband wrote in a letter,

> Our missionary desire is to have God humble our pride so that with broken hearts we surrender to God's sovereign missionary spirit to work grace deeply into our lives. We want his Spirit to teach us how to pray with power, to give us a love for the lost, to enable us to witness with risk-taking boldness and plant churches that are missionary churches. We ourselves grieve over our own sins, which are: (1) fleshly dependence upon secondary means like organization, gift packages, talents, methods, and past experiences rather than relying on the Holy Spirit alone for empowerment; (2) apathy toward the peril of the lost; (3) preoccupation with the "rat race" of modern life; (4) prayerlessness or coldness in prayer; (5) and the greatest evil of all, little passion for Christ and his conquering gospel.

There is a mystery in all of this, but the good news is that God uses the foolish and the needy to accomplish his sovereign work. We need to know that prayer does matter and that when we pray, we are cooperating with God. But what is heaven's perspective?

In Revelation 5 John says, "I began to weep loudly because no one was found worthy to open the scroll or to look into it. And one of the elders said to me, 'Weep no more; behold, the Lion of the tribe of Judah, the Root of David, has conquered'"

(v. 5). When the Lamb is given the scroll, all heaven breaks out in praise: "The four living creatures and the twenty-four elders fell down before the Lamb, each holding a harp, and golden bowls full of incense, which are the prayers of the saints. And they sang a new song" (vv. 8–9). No earthly celebration can compare with the praise of the new song that celebrates the blood of the Lamb that "ransomed people for God from every tribe and language and people and nation" (v. 9).

Prayer matters. Praying for the defeat of the kingdom of darkness, praying for the Spirit to give divine appointments, praying for those who pick up leaflets, praying for the broken lives that Jesus came to heal, praying for dreams—these prayers are collected in that great bowl in heaven, not to be forgotten but to involve heaven in our praying.

We are not left alone in our weakness. There is much at stake as we serve among people who are blinded by the god of this world who keeps them from "seeing the light of the gospel of the glory of Christ" (2 Corinthians 4:4). But we serve and pray in the name of the One who said, "All authority in heaven and on earth has been given to me. Go therefore and make disciples of all nations. . . . And behold, I am with you always, to the end of the age" (Matthew 28:18–20). Go in faith, in partnership with the Lord of heaven and earth, to complete the work he has called us to do.

10

Teaching Others to Pray

Another journey in my life of prayer has been to learn about partnership in prayer—honestly sharing my heart concerns with others and letting them share with me. Whenever Jack and I traveled to speak, he brought an empty notebook, put it on the floor near the pulpit and encouraged people to write their requests and date them. He promised to take their prayers seriously and pray while he was away. He also said that if the request was too private, they could put it on one page and turn to the next blank page for others to write.

On returning from one of our times away, a man came to Jack and thanked him profusely for praying for him. "God answered your prayer for me in more ways than I expected," he said. Jack was intrigued by this and checked back to the date. He found that he had not yet come to that person's request because there had been so many before his. Then it dawned on my husband that the man's act of putting down his plea for prayer was an act of humility. God saw it and was pleased. The young man probably did not know who or where to go to with his problem, and this was his opportunity to go to a safe place.

Since there were many trips, there were many requests. We saw God answer again and again. The decision to ask others to pray for us strengthens our faith and theirs as well.

BUILDING FAITH THROUGH PRAYER

I have a friend in London. When I met her she was clinically depressed. She had been hospitalized and on medication for her depression, but the medication was not helping. Knowing why she was depressed didn't help either. After spending some time listening to her, I suggested that she ask five people (or as many people as she could trust) to pray for her every day for a month. I encouraged her to put her request in a letter, telling them why she wanted them to pray for her.

Jack and I then had to leave the country so I didn't see her for six weeks. When I saw her again, she had a big smile on her face and so did her husband. I asked her to tell me what happened and what she had learned. She said, "I learned that I could trust people to pray for me and that God would answer their prayers. I know that I can pray for others and that God will answer my prayers." The severe depression lifted. This happened six years ago. Last year I saw her again and she was doing well.

On another occasion I sat in the living room of a man who worked in a bank. He had been deeply depressed for nine months. He would wake up every morning angry at God. I suggested he write some people and ask them to pray for him every day for a month. Within two weeks, the depression began to lift. He wrote, "I think I am about back to where I was last fall when this trying period began. I've stopped my morbid introspection and have a positive outlook on life once again."

I have found that when people ask others to pray, the first thing the Spirit does is begin to lift the fog of unbelief. Then he shows them why they are depressed or fearful about life. Jesus said that "he [the Spirit] will convict the world concerning sin" (John 16:8). The Spirit also reveals the work of Christ so the heart can be renewed.

If you feel alone and powerless, I encourage you to write to at least five people, tell them as far as you know what your real problems are, and ask them to pray for you every day for several weeks. Then see what the Spirit does. He is *for* you in a very personal way. He will teach you how to live in the freedom that was bought for you when Jesus died and rose again.

DANIEL'S PRAYERS

Living in exile in Babylon, Daniel was no stranger to his need for prayer, and he found out how important the prayers of his friends were when he was faced with death. Nebuchadnezzar, the king, had a dream that troubled him. He sent for magicians, enchanters, and sorcerers to reveal the dream and its interpretation. The penalty for failure was death. Of course, the magicians insisted that no one could do what the king asked. The king's response was to order them all to be killed. This would have included Daniel. When Daniel heard about the edict, he asked the king for time that he might show him the dream and the interpretation.

"Then Daniel went to his house and made the matter known

to Hananiah, Mishael, and Azariah, his companions, and told them to seek mercy from the God of heaven concerning this mystery, so that Daniel and his companions might not be destroyed with the rest of the wise men of Babylon" (Daniel 2:17–18). God showed Daniel the dream and its meaning. The result was that the king finally knew that Daniel's "God is God of gods and Lord of kings" (2:47). This was the outcome of a "simple" act of going to friends and asking God to do the impossible. God answered, and the world took notice.

I learned to keep this pattern after Jack died. Jack had been my constant prayer partner. A very important part of my life was lost when he died. I knew I would not make it if I did not have friends who would consistently pray for me. I have come to my list of friends many times with a heavy heart, impossible burdens to bear, decisions needing to be made, depression I cannot shake, or loneliness of heart in missing Jack. In response to their prayers, God has met me again and again. The apostle Paul speaks of his reliance on the prayers of others. Though he felt he had "received the sentence of death. But that was to make us rely not on ourselves but on God who raises the dead . . . . On him we have set our hope that he will deliver us again. You also must help us by prayer, so that many will give thanks on our behalf for the blessing granted us through the prayers of many" (2 Corinthians 1:9–11).

PRAYER PARTNERS

I try to take a prayer partner with me whenever I speak at retreats or conferences. Several times I brought along my granddaughter Kimiko. This was an exciting way to bond with her. One morning I was at a prayer meeting at our home in Jenkintown.

I asked the women to pray for a talk I had to give. I said, "I feel like my thoughts are beads rolling around on the floor. I need your prayers to connect my thoughts." But when I went upstairs to write, I still sensed a heavy spirit. My mentally challenged sister, Barbara, seemed to have a direct line to heaven, so I asked her to pray for me. She did, and the words just flowed onto the page.

I often ask friends to pray when my heart seems distant from God. One morning in London, my heart was troubled. A woman had been coming to the house day after day, complaining and expecting us to meet her needs. I was seriously annoyed with her, and at one point I was rude. I had no power to change my attitude, so I asked a young Asian convert whom I had been mentoring to pray for me. She was amazed that I, her teacher, would ask her to pray. But God answered her prayer on my behalf, and this gave her confidence that God would hear her prayers.

At our house in London a Tuesday evening Bible study and prayer meeting provides another opportunity to lay our burdens before one another. On Wednesdays, we meet in Balvinder's home where our Asian friends feel safe to share burdens they can't share with their families. We also have a prayer meeting for women in our home on Friday mornings. I don't go to so many prayer meetings because I am so holy but because I am so needy. It's much easier to be an intercessor when you pray with others. These are times of building friendship and partnering in prayer for God's kingdom to go forward against the kingdom of darkness. I do my "best" praying in community, whether in person, via e-mail, or over the phone. As we pray together, God is making us into "a house of prayer for the nations."

When I am in the United States, I go to WHM on Tuesday mornings for prayer—not only to pray for others, but also to receive their prayers. I struggle with jet lag, and the time changes and my tiredness and weariness can last for weeks. One Tuesday soon after returning to help care for my sister, I did not feel like going to pray. I sensed the Spirit quietly impressing on my heart, "This is where I am." I went. It turned out to be a special time to pray for a young family going to Uganda. My heart was stirred by what they would be facing, and when I prayed for them all my tiredness and self-centeredness left. God met me as I prayed for them.

I don't have the last word on prayer; I only know I am helpless without friends who pray. My son writes, "I do my best parenting in prayer." He has six children, one of whom is severely disabled. How else are our children going to stand against the pressures of the culture and the lure of the Evil One?

Jesus said, "Again I say to you, if two of you agree on earth about anything they ask, it will be done for them by my Father in heaven. For where two or three are gathered in my name, there am I among them" (Matthew 18:19–20). What more can I ask than to know that Jesus not only hears but is among us? Our prayers and petitions of the heart will be answered by our Father in heaven.

We live in a world broken by sin and under the rule of Satan. We groan as we witness the horrible, evil acts of men under the dominion of the Evil One. But the Spirit also groans; he intercedes with groanings too deep for words according to the will of God (Romans 8:26). This is why all things work together for good because the Trinity is involved in our praying. We are not alone. We are partners together in a kingdom that cannot be shaken.

11

Kingdom Praying:
In Step with the Spirit

⌒

I cannot talk about keeping in step with the Spirit without talking about Christ, nor can I talk about Christ without talking about keeping in step with the Spirit. Keeping in step with the Spirit is knowing where the Spirit is going and what he is doing. It is too easy to follow our own plans and find our hearts going astray.

The prayer Jesus taught his disciples to pray begins, "Our Father in heaven, hallowed be your name. Your kingdom come" (Matthew 6:9–10). In this prayer Jesus is inviting us to participate in the advancement of his kingdom. We are in step with the Spirit when we pray that prayer with him. To pray that our Father's name be hallowed and that his kingdom comes should be uppermost in our praying. How does God want to use our mind, feet, hands, and heart to push back the kingdom of darkness?

Notice that when Jesus taught the disciples this prayer, he added a story about a man who needed bread to feed a midnight visitor (Luke 11:1–13). He goes to a neighbor who is reluctant to help, but who finally gives him as much as he needs. Jesus applied the story to our need to ask, seek, and knock for the Holy Spirit if we are to pray as he taught us to pray. It was Jesus' way of telling his disciples that they are helpless to pray without the Spirit.

Jesus knew his disciples would never make it in their own strength. He knew they would be fearful—betraying him, denying him, and running away in his hour of deepest need. He knew they would cower in fear of the authorities after he was crucified.

They needed both assurance (a "guarantee or pledge") and *reas-surance* (the "action of removing someone's doubts or fears"). Jesus gave them both: the sure *promise* that he would not abandon them and the Spirit sent into their hearts as *proof* they were not alone.

CHRIST'S SURRENDERED LIFE OF PRAYER

Jesus told his disciples that another Helper would come to be with them forever. Jesus said, "I will not leave you as orphans; I will come to you" (John 14:18). He also said, "It is to your advantage that I go away, for if I do not go away, the Helper will not come to you. But if I go, I will send him to you" (John 16:7). He gave many more promises on the theme that they would not be alone. He was with them now and would be with them forever.

But their minds were elsewhere. They had just celebrated the Passover and heard words that mystified them:

- "One of you will betray me, one who is eating with me" (Mark 14:18).

- "You will all fall away because of me this night" (Matthew 26:31).
- "This is my blood of the covenant, which is poured out for many for the forgiveness of sins" (Matthew 26:28).
- "[Peter] before the rooster crows, you will deny me three times" (Matthew 26:34).

When they came to the Mount of Olives Jesus said to them,

- "Sit here while I pray" (Mark 14:32).
- "Watch and pray that you may not enter into temptation" (Matthew 26:41).
- "My soul is very sorrowful, even to death; remain here, and watch with me" (Matthew 26:38).
- "Abba, Father, all things are possible for you. Remove this cup from me. Yet not what I will, but what you will" (Mark 14:36).
- "Watch and pray that you may not enter into temptation. The spirit indeed is willing, but the flesh is weak" (Mark 14:38).

Watch what? Watch what genuine discipleship is. Watch what true surrender is. Watch what true prayer is. This is why the disciples needed to listen to what Jesus said to them on the way to the cross.

Watch and pray against what temptation? The temptation to deny, to run, to sleep. Jesus knew what was ahead. Peter especially had not listened; he had even rebuked Jesus for saying he was going to suffer and die.

Peter had been with Jesus from the beginning. He had heard the words, "The kingdom of God is at hand; repent and believe in the gospel" (Mark 1:15). But when the time of testing came, Peter could not pray, he could not watch, he could not believe.

After the resurrection, when Jesus returned to heaven, he sent his Spirit as he had promised. The disciples who hadn't known how to "watch and pray" became mighty men of prayer when the Spirit was given at Pentecost. They certainly didn't act like orphans when they prayed. But despite the fact that we know all this, we often still have a hard time believing that we are not orphans. Somehow we think we have to figure out life's problems on our own, depending on our own resources, forgetting how helpless we are without a total dependence on the Spirit to keep us in step with Christ and to teach us to pray.

In the garden of Gethsemane when Jesus prayed, "Not as I will, but as you will" (Matthew 26:39), he was praying as he taught his disciples to pray: "Thy kingdom come, thy will be done." Jesus lived the Lord's Prayer. He relied completely on his heavenly Father. His passion was for God's glory. He knew he had come into this world to make us right with God. He knew God required this sacrifice to satisfy his justice, and Jesus could not, would not, disobey his Father. But still it was a struggle for him to pray, "Not as I will, but as you will." He knew the cost; he knew he would be separated from his Father. There was silence when Jesus cried on the cross, "Why have you forsaken me?" (Mark 15:34). But it was during those hours that his blood secured eternal redemption for us.

We too need to learn to watch, wait, and keep awake amid the sorrows and struggles we face. Sometimes in the midst of affliction, temptation, and heartache, we come to the place where we too cry out to God to let the cup pass. "If it is possible, please let this cup go away." To hear God say No is painful. But God has a right to say No. God said No to his Son.

PERSONAL SURRENDER TO GOD'S PURPOSE

I stood at my husband's bedside at a hospital in Spain where his health was declining after major heart surgery. I cried to God, "Please let him live!" Let this cup pass. But God took Jack to his heavenly home the next day. God had said No to my prayer for his life. There was now a big hole in my world, a hole that through time only Christ could fill.

It has been a struggle. Many times since Jack died, I have felt alone, even while living with family. These are times when I have failed to watch and pray, times when I have not surrendered to God's will. I believe prayer starts with a deep heart surrender to God—to his plans, his purposes, his will—and a total trust in the Holy Spirit to bring to completion that for which we ask.

"Thy kingdom come" is a powerful prayer. It changes what you live for and what you trust in. I remember being deeply troubled as Jack and I left Uganda in 1979 after three months of ministry. The evil, the chaos, the brokenness at every level had taken a toll on me. At the time, I didn't know enough about the power and presence of the Holy Spirit to cope with what I saw and heard. But God would use that to teach me to pray.

When I asked my husband, "Why couldn't I cope?" he challenged me. "Rose Marie, you act as if the Spirit never came to be your helper, your teacher, and guide. You don't think he can do anything for you."

He was right. I repented, and a few months later I was able to return to Uganda with joy. Nothing in the country had changed—but I had. During that second trip I got malaria, heard devastating news from home, but kept my joy. That is the power of repentance and faith in the Holy Spirit to do what I could not do in my own strength.

THE SPIRIT'S FRUIT OF LOVE

I'm sorry to say I have had to repent again and again of not trusting the Holy Spirit to be my teacher, mentor, guide, and helper. I so easily turn to self—self-trust, self-reliance, self-analysis, and self-seeking.

Relying on self is the enemy of keeping in step with the Spirit. When Jesus told his disciples to "watch and pray," he reminded them that "the spirit is indeed willing, but the flesh is weak" (Matthew 26:41). Love is the first fruit of the Spirit, and here is where I fail again and again. We cannot keep in step with the Spirit if we do not love God and love the world as he loved it.

In the early 1980s, Jack and I were preparing to return to Uganda for the fourth time. I was reading a biography of a young woman, Florence Allshorn, who had gone to Uganda in the 1920s to help in a school for girls. She was twenty-two years old. Her older colleague, a leader at the school, refused to speak to her. She did not help her with the language and basically left her alone. One day Florence was sitting outside the students' dorm, crying and considering a return to England. An old African matron came to her and said, "I have been on this station for fifteen years and I have seen you come out, all of you saying you have brought to us a Savior, but I have never seen this situation saved yet." Florence said, "It brought me to my senses with a bang. . . . I prayed as I have never prayed in my life for one thing"[1]—that I would know and have in me the love of Jesus.

It was then that Florence decided that she was going to read 1 Corinthians 13 every day until God's love controlled her heart. She did this, and soon the atmosphere of the school began to change. Her older colleague began to be kind. The girls in the school started to love one another. Florence stayed for four years until a serious illness took her back to England.

But as I read the story I thought, "I could never be like that." It was a whisper from the Evil One. True, I could never be like that on my own, but I could have turned to Jesus and the Holy Spirit to be different. But I didn't. At the end of our time in Uganda I told Jack, "I am never coming back."

And I didn't, until six months later when Jack was again in Uganda and suffered a heart attack. This time I knew I needed the presence of the Spirit and this time I asked for it. My heart was filled with peace as I returned to a country to which I had said I would never return. I lacked the proper documents, and I didn't know if my husband was alive or dead. But after asking for the fullness of the Spirit and the presence of Christ, I arrived with faith and joy. I had no problem entering the country, and Jack was alive.

As I brought my heart before the Lord, I had to face the fact that I wasn't willing to identify with the people in Uganda. And if I had been in the garden with Jesus, I would have slept with the others. All of that was true, but *that's not all the truth there is.* When I also remember that I am an adopted daughter of the living God and that by the Spirit I can cry Abba Father, my heart is at peace. I can move out into the world with confidence that I am not alone.

KEEPING IN STEP WITH THE SPIRIT IN OUR WEAKNESS

How do you pray "Thy kingdom come" when bombs go off in Mumbai, and when Christians are persecuted in Orissa? How do you face the heartache when your firstborn son is born dead as my grandson and his wife experienced? When an elderly man weeps at the death of his wife after sixty-four years? When a teenager gives birth and then risks losing her child because of her own foolish actions? When a mother loses a son who was the light of her life? You have your list of unfathomable heartaches too.

N. T. Wright says, "At any given moment, someone we know is facing darkness and horror: illness, death, bereavement, torture, catastrophe, loss. . . . And when we ourselves find the ground giving way beneath our feet, as sooner or later we shall, Gethsemane is where to go. That is where we find that the Lord of the world, to whom is now committed all authority (Matthew 28:18), has been there before us."[2]

Jennifer Myhre, a missionary doctor in the mountains of Uganda, wrote in a prayer letter:

> A loving Father did miraculously remove the final cup of judgment, did set in motion a re-creation in which the garden of Gethsemane will become the Garden of Heaven. But the path he gave to Jesus led through the cross. We strive toward the humility of this prayer, this emptying of our way of transformation and this acceptance of God's way to change the world. As Jesus committed himself, he taught us that the midnight garden was not the final reality, that he and we can trust God to be at work behind the scenes. For today, for this week and this year, we pour ourselves into the cross-walk laid out in front of us, trusting that eventually it will come together for good.

So we pray, "Thy kingdom come." Satan and death are defeated enemies. Jesus came as a Lamb crucified on a cross. This is the only way we or the world can be fixed. We are sons and daughters of the living God. God sent the Spirit of his Son into our hearts crying, "Abba Father." We are called to go out into the world with his message. Keeping in step with the Spirit, we go, but never alone, for him who died for us and rose again.

12

Paul's Prayers

In our work in Southall, we are regularly reminded of the requirements of the different faiths within the Asian community. For example, one requirement for a Muslim is to pray five times a day. What benefit does he receive for this? He can feel good that he has done his duty, though it may not touch his heart.

There are many rituals involved in the worship of Hindu gods, including ceremonial washings, putting a mark on yourself, and ringing a bell to let the gods know you are there. The gods promise protection and help in response to your requests. If you are a Sikh, you must recite a mantra, follow a ritual of prayers, and pray in a *gurdwara*, a Sikh temple, for the needs of your family. There is a need to demonstrate how devout you are.

Our world of praying is turned upside down when we read how the apostle Paul prayed for others. One of his prayers is included in his letter to the church at Ephesus (Ephesians 3:14–19). In the first part of chapter 3, Paul marveled at the unity of the family God created when he brought the Gentiles (us) into the family of God, which had once been comprised only of the Jews. At Masih Gahr, the church our team has planted in Southall, we enjoy each other even though we are from many different cultures. Some visitors to Masih Gahr marvel that this could happen, but it is the work of God. In Paul's time it was also a marvel that Jews and Gentiles would pray together.

If I were writing you a letter from prison as Paul was, I would probably tell you how bad the food was, how nasty the other women were, and how I couldn't get a decent night's sleep. I would ask God why he was angry with me, and what I had done to deserve such treatment. I would ask God to get me out of prison! I could very easily start praying like a Hindu or Muslim: "Give me what *I* think I need." But this isn't how Paul prayed. His prayer is also a prayer for us as a family, a powerful example of how we should pray for one another.

A PRAYER FOR OUR INNER BEING

Paul is interested in our "inner being" (Ephesians 3:16). He prays in verse 17 that "Christ may dwell in your hearts through faith." But isn't Christ already dwelling in our hearts? Paul is asking for more of what we already have. There are so many anxieties, fears, and worries that face us—we need a new infusion of Christ in our hearts every day.

What does it look like to have Christ fill us? What does he want to fill us *with*? Paul prays, "That you, being rooted and grounded in love, may have strength to comprehend with all the saints what is the breadth and length and height and depth, and to know the love of Christ that surpasses knowledge, that you may be filled with all the fullness of God" (3:17–19).

What is Christ's love like? "It is wide enough to embrace the world. . . . long enough to last forever. . . . high enough to take sinners to Heaven. . . . deep enough to take Christ to the very depths to reach the lowest sinner."[1]

This love isn't just for us to enjoy by ourselves. It is what we are meant to share in community. It should be evident in how we treat one another. The giant redwood trees in California are some of the tallest trees in the world. When storms come, they are able to withstand the force of the wind because the root system of every individual tree is intertwined with the roots of the trees around them. That is what Paul is praying for on our behalf: That our inner beings would be rooted in the love of God and interconnected with one another so that others would also be drawn into the community of love God has created.

Here is what Donald Grey Barnhouse wrote about love:

Love is the key.
Joy is love singing.
Peace is love resting.
Long-suffering is love enduring.
Kindness is love touching.
Goodness is love's character.
Faithfulness is love's habit.
Gentleness is love's self-forgetfulness.
Self-control is love holding the reins.[2]

THE VALUE OF LOVE

In his prayers, why did Paul emphasize love? Because in times of trial love is the first quality to be lost. To the Corinthian church, which was struggling with sin, Paul wrote, "But I am afraid that just as Eve was deceived by the serpent's cunning, your minds may somehow be led astray from your sincere and pure devotion to Christ" (2 Corinthians 11:3 NIV). Believing Satan's lies, we are easily deceived into thinking that God doesn't love us.

Paul's emphasis on love was important for another reason. Some thirty years after Paul wrote his second letter to Corinth, Jesus spoke from heaven to the apostle John, who was living in exile for his witness for Christ. Jesus told John to write a letter to the church in Ephesus. Through John, Jesus told the Ephesians they were doing many good things, but he had one thing against them: "You have forsaken your first love. Remember the height from which you have fallen! Repent" (Revelation 2:4–5 NIV). If we veer from devotion to Christ forgetting God's love and failing to love one another, we become prisoners of our own fears, anxieties, circumstances, and the opinions of others. This is a worse prison than anything Paul or John experienced.

All the members of the Godhead—the Trinity—are involved in the prayer Paul prays in Ephesians. In Ephesians 3:16–18, Paul prays that the *Father* "out of his glorious riches he may strengthen [us] with power through his *Spirit* . . . so that *Christ* may dwell in your hearts through faith . . . [that we] may have power, together with all the saints, to grasp how wide and long and high and deep is the love of Christ" (NIV). It goes beyond mere knowledge. It can only be grasped by faith.

This prayer is answered by "him who is able to do immeasurably more than all we ask or imagine, according to his power that is at work within us" (3:20 NIV). It is all God's doing; we believe it by faith.

A PRAYER GOD DID NOT ANSWER

When Paul prays, we can tell that he is looking forward to God's answer. But what happens when we earnestly ask God to change our circumstances and God does not answer as we had hoped?

Paul endured much persecution. He was exposed to death again and again. Five times the Jews lashed him thirty-nine times; he was beaten with rods; he was stoned, shipwrecked three times, and always in danger from both Jews and Gentiles (2 Corinthians 11:23–26).

How did God encourage Paul in all of these trials? Not in the way we might expect. God "caught [him] up to the third heaven" where Paul heard "inexpressible things, things that man is not permitted to tell." Then, "to keep me from becoming conceited because of these surpassingly great revelations, there was given me a thorn in my flesh, a messenger of Satan, to torment me" (2 Corinthians 12:2–7 NIV). We don't know what this thorn was, but it was something Paul found almost impossible to endure.

Paul goes on to say, "Three times I pleaded with the Lord to take it away from me. But he said to me, 'My grace is sufficient for you, for my power is made perfect in weakness' " (2 Corinthians 12:9 NIV). Whatever the problem was, it made Paul weak. Paul wrote that this happened so that he wouldn't be conceited. It is amazing how little he talks about the "paradise experience." Knowing my own heart, that is what I would talk about, but Paul knew that grace is so much more attractive! Paul could now say, "Therefore I will boast all the more gladly about my weaknesses, so that Christ's power may rest on me" (2 Corinthians 12:9). He ends his prayer by saying, "For when I am weak, then I am strong" (v. 10).

In my Bible I have March 27, 1998, written next to 2 Corinthians 12:10. It recalls one of the times since my husband died when I have been keenly aware of how needy and weak I am. Sometimes it is hard to admit this. But when I do, a different kind of strength comes into my life. I find I don't need everything I think I need because when my heart is content with Christ, his power rests on me. I am not always at the place where I delight in insults, weaknesses, hardships, and difficulties, but when I do, I get a greater taste of grace.

We are saved by grace, and we live by grace. We are made alive when God's favor rests on us, and we continue to live by the power and strength of the Spirit, who grants us grace in our weakness. I encourage you to affirm with Paul, "When I am weak, then I am strong."

13

Prayer: The Spiritual Battle

⟶

We are part of a big story. God's kingdom is moving against the kingdom of darkness. One day "the earth will be filled with the knowledge of the glory of the Lord, as the waters cover the sea" (Habakkuk 2:14 NIV). God invites us to participate, through prayer, in his plan to create from every tribe, tongue, and nation a people for his glory. Each of us has a special place in this plan. As we pray and trust in the Holy Spirit, we can make a difference.

We are involved in a battle of cosmic proportions between good and evil. To quote John Piper, "The need of the hour is a global wartime mentality."[1] I wish I had known this when my husband was doing church planting and we were bringing up our family. In the church were people who wanted to control it. At first Jack did not see the work of the Evil One behind this. It was the same with our children. We assumed that if we did everything right, our children would be fine. We did not realize that Satan was sowing weeds among the wheat.

When Jack and I realized that we needed to pray against the powers of darkness for our children and for the church, it changed the way we prayed for ourselves, for other individuals, and for the world. We learned to pray that the Son of God would bind Satan.

WAGING SPIRITUAL WARFARE

Each day we face a battle. Paul reminds us that "we do not wage war the way the world does. The weapons we fight with are not the weapons of the world. On the contrary, they have divine power to demolish strongholds" (2 Corinthians 10:3–4 NIV). "Our struggle is not against flesh and blood, but against the rulers, against the authorities, against the powers of this dark world and against the spiritual forces of evil in the heavenly realms" (Ephesians 6:12 NIV). Paul links the battle with prayer in Ephesians 6:18: "And pray in the Spirit on all occasions with all kinds of prayers and requests. With this in mind, be alert and always keep on praying for all the saints" (NIV).

In our work among South Asians, we need to be alert to Satan's attacks through their cultures. The idols of Hinduism call to mind Paul's words to the Corinthians, "The sacrifices of pagans are offered to demons, not to God" (1 Corinthians 10:20 NIV). On one of my husband's visits to a Hindu temple, a young man was standing before the idols saying, "Why are you trying to kill me?" Paul writes that behind the idols are demons. So we pray against their power and the destructive lies of the Evil One. Muslims are deceived into believing that Christ never went to the cross, so we pray against this satanic lie. In the cultures we encounter, religion, tradition, food, clothes, honor, and loyalty are all designed to keep people from hearing the gospel. In 2 Corinthians Paul writes, "The god of this age has blinded the minds of unbelievers" (2 Corinthians 4:4 NIV). At Masih Gahr we pray that God will build his family so converts who are thrown out of their families will have a place to go. We often pray for their dreams. We have heard stories of Christ appearing to them.

In the midst of spiritual warfare, we want to remember not only our enemy but the triumphant Christ. Lilias Trotter, a missionary to Muslims, wrote, "He shall sit as a priest upon his throne. 'Ask of me and I will give thee [the nations] as thy possession.' What he receives as Priest he dispenses as King and somehow the whole aspect of prayer has been reversed. I used to think that our intercession must sweep round from us to him and back with the answer, but now I see it differently; it all starts with [God] and sweeps down here as low as our helplessness, then back to his throne, the place of power and authority."[2] We can pray with authority for the destruction of Satan's strongholds so that God will claim the inheritance he has given to his Son.

THE BATTLE FOR OUR HEARTS

The battle is fierce. R. Arthur Mathews writes: "In his true character as adversary, Satan is very much alive to rob the finished work of Christ of its full effect among men."[3] The battle is fought not only in cultures but in individual hearts. Mathews continues, "Because of the hostility of the devil, the work of conforming the members of Christ's Body to the likeness of the soldier-image of the Head is high on the priority list of the Holy Spirit. As believers, we are in Christ and He in us. . . . So we are no longer free to play the role of civilians, living as if there were no war."[4]

If our highest expression of worship is to love God with all our heart, soul, mind, and strength, then we know that this is where Satan will attack. He has not changed his strategy since he met our mother Eve. Paul writes in 2 Corinthians 11:3, "But I am afraid that just as Eve was deceived by the serpent's cunning, your minds may somehow be led astray from your sincere and pure devotion to Christ" (NIV).

Often when I know my heart has gone astray, I ask the Spirit to show me how my heart as been seduced by the Evil One. It is difficult to pray if our hearts are cluttered with the concerns of this life, its worries and fears. Often this is where Satan seduces us. One of our missionaries in Dublin talked about "learning to make no agreement with the enemy." That counteracts the enemy's first strategy with Eve, which is to cast doubt on God's goodness and on his character. If he can get you to agree with those lies, he is taking you down and out of the battle.

We are here to do battle for people who are walking in darkness. We need to "be strong in the Lord and in his mighty power" (Ephesians 6:10 NIV). We need to "take [our] stand against the devil's schemes. For our struggle is not against flesh and blood, but against the rulers, against the authorities, against the powers of this dark world and against the spiritual forces of evil in the heavenly realms" (6:11–12 NIV). For this we need "the full armor of God" (v. 11 NIV): the helmet of salvation, the belt of truth, the breastplate of righteousness, our feet shod with preparation of the gospel of peace, the shield of faith to quench all the flaming arrows of the evil one. And above all this, we put on prayer and pray in the Spirit. To pray against the designs of the Evil One, we need the Spirit.

A missionary friend said that for years she listened to the lies of the Evil One that she was a failure. She could never measure up against her mother's accusation that she was a bad daughter for taking her grandchildren so far from home to another country. This missionary knew these words were poison and began to reject them. She took the sword of the Spirit, the Word of God, and lived out of the truth that she is a daughter of the living God. As we pray, the Spirit teaches us. We are praying against the Enemy of the kingdom of light, so remember that the Evil One is the god of this age. He "has blinded the minds of unbelievers, so that they cannot see the light of the gospel of the glory of Christ, who is the image of God" (2 Corinthians 4:4 NIV).

If this is what our Enemy is like, do not underestimate the wiles, seductions and roarings of the Evil One when you struggle. He is always seeking to seduce us from a simple devotion to Christ.

A DISQUIETED HEART

A disquieted heart for me is a red flag. It leads me to ask questions like: Where have I been seduced from my devotion to Jesus? And, to what have I devoted myself that keeps me from loving the One who gave his life for me? I ask the Spirit to show me where my heart has gone astray, and where I have listened to the lies of the Evil One. Then I pray, "Dear Lord, restore me. 'Create in me a clean heart . . . and renew a right spirit within me'" (Psalm 51:10).

In his book *Taking the Christian Life Seriously*, Sinclair Ferguson writes, "While every believer enjoys the ministry of the Spirit as his helper, he also has conflict with Satan as the hinderer.

Indwelling sin in the believer contends with the desires the Spirit plants within him. That is a deep-seated and painful conflict, but it is exacerbated by the fact that it creates a perfect landing place for Satan."[5]

I experienced this at a deep level after Jack died. It was easy for me to lose my bearings, and I became vulnerable to Satan's lies and insinuations. But God knew this and in recent years has continued to dismantle my seeming strength, reorient my priorities, and in return, give me himself. Remember that you are not a victim of your circumstances, the decisions of others, or your own weakness. Your enemy is not your unfulfilled desires, your fellow laborers, or your situation as difficult as these sometimes seem. God has work for you to do. But you do have an enemy. You need to know him and fight him in prayer. I can assure you that there is an abundant supply of the Spirit for the asking.

SATAN'S LIES

Here are some of the lies that turned me inward when I should have been looking outward to engage in the battle for the souls of those who need Christ.

You are alone. This is the biggest lie. I wasn't alone but it felt like it because I chose not to believe the words of Jesus. I was vulnerable to thinking that I had to somehow make it on my own. I had to be God. Like Eve, I followed my impressions instead of the words of Christ who said, "I will never leave you nor forsake you" (Hebrews 13:5), and "I will ask the Father, and he will give you another Helper, to be with you forever" (John 14:16). I needed to repent daily of being seduced from a simple and pure devotion to Christ and instead to know and rely on the promises of God.

You don't measure up. Trying to manufacture an identity from others or from ministry is deadly to the conscience. Lorraine Smith, a former missionary to Uganda, wrote: "Team members work closely together. We observe each other's strengths and weaknesses. We either feel inferior and cover up self or superior and display our selves. Our pride keeps us from taking the lowest place." I had to put aside selfish ambition to consider others better than myself. I needed to repent of my pride and my drifting from Christ. I again had to go to Christ to be renewed in my identity in him.

You are not worthy. When Jack and I first went to Uganda, I was overwhelmed by the devastation I saw. Many times I thought, "What am I doing here?" Yet through those times I learned how trustworthy Christ is. I learned the beauty of forgiveness at the Communion table. My heart's self-trust was uncovered so that I could finally listen to the Spirit tell me that I wasn't an orphan. This is when the Spirit speaks to us—in the dark, lonely, seemingly God-forsaken times.

In his book *Following Jesus,* N. T. Wright says:

> We know ourselves to be Easter people, called to minister to a world full of Calvarys. In that knowledge we find that the hand that dries *our* tears passes the cloth on to us, and bids us follow him, to go and dry one another's tears. The Lamb calls us to follow him wherever he goes; into the dark places of the world, the dark places of our own hearts, the places where tears blot out the sunlight, the places where tyrants pave the grass with concrete; and he bids us shine his morning light into the darkness, and share his ministry of wiping away the tears."6

Who *is* worthy? When we come to the end of our excuses, blame shifting, judgmentalism, complaining, and boasting, we are confronted with the only One who is worthy. Read the song in Revelation 5:12–14, which we will someday sing together with the created world: "Worthy is the Lamb, who was slain, to receive power and wealth and wisdom and strength and honor and glory and praise! . . . To him who sits on the throne and to the Lamb be praise and honor and glory and power, for ever and ever! . . . Amen" (NIV).

How can we connect with these truths to fight the battle before us? We need to repent of our sins, put on the armor of God, humble ourselves to consider others better than ourselves, and pray. But we can do all these things and still struggle.

THE LOVE THAT CASTS OUT FEAR

Recently I had a long dry spell, convinced that I was unworthy to be in London. Something was missing. I called trusted friends and asked them to pray against the lies and designs of the Evil One. I also took a day away from the house to wait upon the Lord. Since I live with eight other people, it is not always easy for me to be quiet in my heart at home. I was in a bookstore and picked up a copy of N. T. Wright's *Following Jesus*. As I read, the Spirit began to work. I realized that I was missing what I always ask people to pray for—a simple and pure devotion to Christ. I also knew that I didn't know Christ and the power of his resurrection deep in my heart. I knew the facts but I had lost the music.

We can talk about unworthiness and feeling alone, but it won't help much if we don't know that behind all the excuses is fear. There are more commands in the Bible to not be afraid than any other command—and for good reason. We are afraid we won't measure up, afraid we will fail, afraid that God's plans aren't good for us or our children, or (as singles) afraid we won't get married. We are afraid that evil is more powerful than the resurrected Christ. We are afraid that the promises of God are not for us, and so on.

While all this was going on in my heart, these words intruded: "If you knew the gift of God and who it is that asks you for a drink, you would have asked him and he would have given you living water" (John 4:10 NIV). I remembered that these are the words Jesus said to a thirsty, needy woman one hot day by a well. But I also realized that he was speaking to me.

"Rose Marie, if you only knew that I had living water all the time, you wouldn't have to drink at empty cisterns of self-worth. You only need to come and drink of me, the fountain of living water. If only you knew that God has 'rescued [you] from the dominion of darkness and brought [you] into the kingdom of the Son he loves, in whom [you] have redemption, the forgiveness of sins' (Colossians 1:13–14 NIV), then you would be filled with joy. If you only knew that 'perfect love casts out fear' (1 John 4:18)." After exposing the Samaritan woman's deeper thirsts, Jesus revealed himself to her with these words: "I who speak to you am he" (John 4:26). And so he met me also.

FOLLOWING JESUS

I now have a deeper hunger to know Jesus and the power of his resurrection. Jesus has trodden the path before us. He has inaugurated the new covenant, bringing the age-old plan of God to its fulfillment. Jesus is the final sacrifice, the One who has done for us what we could not do for ourselves; the One who lived our life and died our death, and now ever lives to make intercession for us. And now we go out gladly to follow Jesus to the broken and needy—to the ones who are thirsty and don't know it; to the ones who think their lives are hopelessly broken; to the ones who need to hear the words of Jesus, "I am the resurrection and the life" (John 11:25).

> As we ourselves open our lives to the warmth of [God's] love, we begin to lose our fear; and as we begin to lose our fear, we begin to become people through whom the power of that love can flow out into the world around that so badly needs it. That is an essential part of what it means to follow Jesus. And as the power of that love replaces the love of power, so in a measure, anticipating the last great day, God's kingdom comes, and God's will is done, on earth as it is in heaven. We will not see the work accomplished in all its fullness until the last day. But we will, in following Jesus, be both implementing his work and hastening that day.[7]

This is our true calling. Do not let Satan hinder. Do not let fear and unbelief keep you from your true calling to be salt and light in this dark world. Pray, believe, and go!

14

Praying the Psalms

I was married to a theologian, and much of my view of God came through the grid of doctrine. The incredible truths I learned in books like Romans and Galatians shaped my heart to understand the gospel and grace in a deeper way. I am forever thankful for this. Studying those books also prepared me to learn truth about God in a more personal way.

That is when I went to the Psalms. At different times, my heart was led by the Spirit to make different psalms my daily prayer. They continue to impact my heart with their honesty, laments, and cries for help as I use them in my prayer life. They call me to remember my need for an undivided heart, to remember the steadfast love of God, and to remember that he is faithful. Here are some of the psalms that have had the most impact on me and my prayer life.

PSALM 119

A few years ago, I was disturbed by how little impact God's Word seemed to have on my life. The Word of God is a double-edged sword, but it seemed like a putty knife—not very effective except to keep a window in place. That's when I first thought maybe the Psalms would help.

For years I had avoided Psalm 119 as too long and repetitious. But now I turned to it, asking God to humble my heart, teach me, and lead my heart away from coldness to a warmhearted devotion to his will, his thoughts, and his ways. I reasoned that if there are 157 verses, there must be something here I needed to learn! The psalm has twenty-two sections, which I started praying through one per day. Did I always sense a connection to God after doing this? No. However, I knew I would not survive a busy ministry life without the Spirit teaching me through his Word.

What did I find as I studied Psalm 119?

- God delights in a heart given to him without reservation.
- The writer sees himself as weak and needy. I often feel the same.
- There is strength for the journey.
- There is comfort in affliction.
- The Word is a guide for each day.
- There is an eternal perspective on life.
- God's Word gives light, keeps from sin, and gives hope.

Most important, I found Christ. When Jesus appeared to his doubting disciples after his resurrection, he said, "Everything written about me in the Law of Moses and the Prophets and the Psalms must be fulfilled" (Luke 24:44). I began to pray through this psalm in that light, wanting it to teach me more about Jesus' thoughts, his words, and his relationship to his Father.

These perspectives did not come to me at first. After praying through the psalm once, I figured I did not need to pray through it again. Big mistake! My heart kept drifting. So I prayed through the psalm again, and then again, until it became a daily habit. I read other Scriptures regularly, but I still pray through one section a day, sometimes two, and now it has become my heart's prayer.

This psalm is convicting. When I read verses like verse 20, "My soul is consumed with longing for your rules at all times," I know I do not feel that way, but I want to. Then it becomes a prayer of repentance. It also brings me to Jesus, who never wavered from the desires of his Father's heart.

Verses 129 to 136 are a plea to keep my steps steady and to let no sin have dominion over my life. It is a prayer for God's face to shine upon me. Next to these verses I have penned five dates, reminding me of times and places when I needed these words of instruction, guidance, hope, and comfort.

Not long ago I returned from a trip to Chattanooga and Nashville, Tennessee, where I spoke on God's faithfulness to his promises. I challenged men and women to rest their faith on a kingdom that cannot be shaken. I met with young mothers with many fears as they raise their children. It was a special time. But when I returned home to help care for my disabled sister, I had crises of my own. My daughter, who is my sister's primary caregiver, was not well. I wrenched my arm pulling up the bars of my sister's bed, and the bathroom renovation to accommodate her wheelchair was not yet completed. On top of that there were taxes to be paid and writing to do. I was not at peace.

Again I turned to Psalm 119: "Great peace have those who

love your law" (v. 165). "All my ways are before you" (v. 168). "I have gone astray like a lost sheep; seek your servant" (v. 176). My heart rested when I read these words. I could not solve the problems or change my circumstances, but I could ask God to redirect my heart to trust in his steadfast love.

There is so much more to ponder and pray over in this psalm. If you take a section a day and pray through it in earnest prayer, you will find (vv. 98–100):

- God's commandment makes you "wiser than [your] enemies."
- You have "more understanding than all [your] teachers."
- You "understand more than the aged."

I pray Psalm 119 not out of desperation, but with thankfulness, asking God to search my heart, expose self-centeredness, and lead me to a quiet rest in his steadfast love. I encourage you to do the same.

PSALM 121

There are other psalms that quiet the heart, especially in times of uncertainty. A few years ago while in London, I began to have trouble eating. I was losing weight and did not know why. I came back to the United States for a granddaughter's wedding, and my doctor quickly scheduled tests. Tumors were discovered and cancer was suspected.

Now Psalm 121 became a reality. Like the psalmist, I had questions. Am I going to go through what Jack went through when he had cancer? Will I be able to return to London? I remembered the first indication that something was wrong with Jack. His abdomen swelled and an x-ray showed a large growth in his stomach. It was painful to hear the news, "You have cancer." The memory of all Jack went through was still vivid after twenty-seven years: going through chemo, losing his appetite, his strength, and his hair, and spending long days in the hospital. All that rushed back when I heard the doctor say to me, "You have tumors growing in your stomach."

As the psalmist wrote, I wondered, "From where does my help come?" (v. 1). My question was legitimate, but my heart needed to be settled on eternal truth, not the immediate future. Surgery was scheduled. My children gathered around my hospital bed. I asked my son to read Psalm 121: "My help comes from the LORD, who made heaven and earth" (v. 2). I needed those words at that moment. Would God keep my foot from slipping? Would God stay awake during the operation? Each question was answered in this psalm with a resounding Yes.

The doctor came into my room and listened as my son prayed through the psalm with me. Five hours later, still groggy, all I wanted to hear was God speaking to my heart. The tumors turned out to be cancer, but they were growing on the lining of the stomach. Since they did not invade the stomach itself, there was no need for further treatment.

God did not sleep. God was the shade on my right hand. He kept me from evil. I know it does not always happen this way for those who suffer from cancer, but the truth of the psalm remains the same no matter the outcome.

God continues to keep my feet. In London my room is on the second floor. It is the same in the United States. So, many times a day, I walk up and down the stairs and pray, "Lord, do not let my foot slip." (I also hold onto the railing!) When I am driving,

I ask God to be on my right and left—keeping me from hurting anyone. It is an all-day prayer, not just for me, but for my family and the world that is slipping into a Christ-less eternity.

I have a disabled granddaughter. When she was going to school, her mother knew when she would be walking up and down the stairs. She prayed this psalm, "God, keep her feet from falling." God did.

This is a psalm about a caring, watchful God—the God who made heaven and earth, who watches over our feet, who is our shade, who keeps us from evil, and takes note of our comings and goings.

Psalm 121 brings to mind the words of Isaiah: "How beautiful upon the mountains are the feet of him who brings good news, who publishes peace, who brings good news of happiness, who publishes salvation, who says to Zion, 'Your God reigns'" (Isaiah 52:7). My feet have walked around potholes in Uganda, along dusty roads in India, and through cluttered streets in Southall into homes where needy widows live, bringing good news: God does indeed reign.

PSALM 51

The Spirit uses the Psalms to engage the heart on multiple levels. Psalm 119 engages the indifferent heart, Psalm 121 the fearful heart. In Psalm 51, God reminds me that I need a complete *change* of heart like David. He was a man in the wrong place at the wrong time, napping on his rooftop when he should have been out fighting God's enemies, securing the border of his kingdom. Not being where he should have been, he let his eyes wander. His heart soon followed and desired what did not belong to him. He asked a question, "Who is she?" He gave a command. "Bring her here." She conceived, her pregnancy was covered up with her husband's murder, and God was not pleased.

When Nathan the prophet exposed David's heart with the story of a stolen lamb, David cried out that he had sinned against the Lord. He was told that God despised what he had done. He had "utterly scorned the LORD" (2 Samuel 12:14).

Cut to the heart, David writes, "Have mercy on me, O God, according to your steadfast love. . . . blot out my transgressions. . . . I know my transgressions, and my sin is ever before me. Against you, you only, have I sinned and done what is evil in your sight" (Psalm 51:1–4). He had deeply wronged Bathsheba in causing her to commit adultery and then robbed her *and* her husband by arranging Uriah's murder. He knew there was no one else in the universe who could forgive, restore, and renew his heart. In Psalm 32:4, we read that God's hand was heavy upon him day and night, a huge burden to bear as he dealt with the guilt of his sin.

I am no different. I, too, have a heart that easily departs from the Living God. I have inked in many dates next to this psalm in my Bible and I keep adding more. How does my heart drift? Like David, like God's people who rebelled against entering the Promised Land, my problems start with "a sinful, unbelieving heart that turns away from the living God" (Hebrews 3:12 NIV). When I am discontented, lack compassion, judge, seek praise instead of God's glory, make my own plans, or lean on my own understanding, my heart has already started to drift. This is when I cry out with David, "Create in me a clean heart, O God, and renew a right spirit within me" (51:10).

I have many entries in my journal that record my prayers through this psalm.

- "Have mercy according to your steadfast love. Blot out my many sins. You know what they are: the deep roots of unbelief, the branches of self-centeredness that choke the Word. Dig deep, Lord!"
- "Wash me thoroughly and completely. I know you desire a heart that has been cleansed from leaning on my own understanding instead of living for your glory. In the innermost part of my heart, the secret heart that no one knows but you, teach me wisdom."
- "Lord, I have lost my joy. Create in me a clean heart, just as you created the heavens and the earth. You know the superficial motives of my heart; uphold me with a willing spirit. You know I have been doing a lot of teaching. Now teach *me*, and then the hearts of the women."

How hard it is to come to the place where I accept God's evaluation of what is important, to believe that a broken and contrite heart is what pleases him. It is too easy for me to live for the applause and approval of others and forget what pleases God.

David knew the importance of the burnt offerings that were offered daily at the temple for sin. But he also knew that a greater David was to come, who would give his life's blood for the sins of his people. I know there is nothing I can do to make my heart sing when I am overwhelmed by my sin. I too come to Jesus for cleansing, renewal, and restoration because royal blood was shed for me two thousand years ago.

This psalm is a heart's appeal for forgiveness. David's sin was serious and he was severely disciplined. The baby died. But when he took Bathsheba as his wife, she gave birth to Solomon, one of the great kings of Israel. God never wastes anything. Even our sin is used in a mysterious way for his glory.

Oh, the sweet joy when the heart is renewed, delivered from the relentless pursuit of approval and a self-centered life! What a joy to find life in Christ alone, knowing God is pleased with a broken and contrite heart. This is my daily prayer.

PSALM 131

But my heart is not always at rest. There are many voices: duties, obligations, and responsibilities. I have expectations as to what I should do, what I would like to do, and what others think I should do, completely forgetting what pleases God. Psalm 131 speaks to this unrest.

About a year ago, I was getting ready to take the train to the Philadelphia airport. I had anything but a quiet heart. My book project needed to be worked on; decisions needed to be made concerning my sister; home renovations were stalled; and I wanted to return to London. As I was leaving the house, I said something that revealed a thankless heart. Guilt and condemnation ruled.

I began to pray through Psalm 131, but I could not make my heart still. Arriving at the ticket counter, I gave the attendant my ID and money to pay for my extra luggage. Without my realizing it, she put my ID into the change drawer. When I was ready to go through security, I couldn't find it, and they were not going to let me on the plane without it.

I went back to the counter, and it was found in the change drawer. But my plane was leaving at a distant terminal. Could I make it in time? It was a long walk, but I made the flight. Finally, sitting next to the window on the plane, I began to read through Psalm 131.

"O LORD, my heart is not lifted up; my eyes are not raised too

high" (v. 1). The Spirit gently showed me the pride of my heart: wanting to please my daughter and editor and not doing a very good job with either, which was evidenced in a thankless attitude. He showed me my presumption. I acted like a horse that has to be held in with bit and bridle, rather than quietly waiting on the Lord for my return to London.

"I do not occupy myself with things too great and too marvelous for me" (v. 1). I was preoccupied with the future. In my pride, I wanted to figure out what God was doing so I could get on with my life. God wanted me to be content to go slow in the writing and to wait until matters were resolved with my sister.

There are other matters that occupy us: fear, an uncertain future, sickness, disabilities, anxieties, worries about children, money, relationships, hurts, rejections, the economy, reputation, and unfulfilled longings to name a few.

"But I have calmed and quieted my soul, like a weaned child with its mother; like a weaned child is my soul within me" (v. 2). A weaned child is not grasping for her mother's milk. She can sit quietly on her lap, satisfied. She still needs her mother but in a different way. She is free to grow, to learn, to play, and to develop relationships.

This is where God finally brought me as the plane began to descend. I let go of the future and my pride. I rested like a weaned child in my Father's wise plan.

"O [Rose Marie], hope in the LORD *from this time forth and forevermore"* (v. 3). Now my hope was in the LORD—his will, his way, and not my own. It is not an easy place to come to or to stay in, but it is the place of rest.

I prayed, "Father, forgive me for putting my agenda before your will. Forgive a heart that is proud and restless. Forgive me for not quietly waiting until your will is made plain. Forgive me for not having a thankful heart for all your blessings and mercies. Thank you for not leaving me alone; for sending your Spirit to teach, lead, guide, and instruct in the way you choose. Thank you for the blessings of a calm, quieted soul. This is truly what you have done. Please, dear Father, do not let me go on in pride. Continue to show me where and when I go astray."

There is one more way God quieted my soul during this experience. The woman who brought me my change at the ticket counter looked at me and said, "Do you remember me?" I did not. She said, "I am Mary. You took me in when I was a troubled teenager." Leaning over the counter, we hugged each other. She apologized for leaving the way she had. She was now married with children and working as an airline ticket agent. Even though my heart had not yet been quieted, God showed me that my labor so many years before had not been in vain.

My pride was a major hindrance to a quiet heart. All the day's pressures had shown me this. Not everyone who reads this will have the same set of circumstances, but it is wise to ask the Spirit to show you why your heart is restless and dissatisfied with the events of your life. Ask him to bring you to that quiet place "near to the heart of God."[1]

PSALM 139

When my heart is in turmoil, when people disappoint and circumstances are out of control, I can find it difficult to express my feelings. Then it is time to turn to a psalm and ask God to help me understand his ways and the ways of my heart. Psalm 139 reminds me that I serve a very personal God who knows my thoughts and my ways and wants me, in turn, to know his.

Its author is David—shepherd, warrior, singer, and king. I can learn much from the rises and falls of his life as he always brings me back to a humble submission to the God he loved and served.

One scholar notes, "The Psalms assign great value to us as children of God. At the same time, they humble mankind as of little consequence beside the greatness of the Almighty. They give comfort in sorrow, yet severely rebuke sin. Most wonderful of all, they celebrate redemption by the mercy of God."[2]

Psalm 139 speaks to my heart struggles in this wonderfully balanced way. In the first six verses, God expresses his intimate knowledge of who I am.

- He searches and knows me. His searching is active and personal. The word for "searching" is based on the word for winnowing wheat, separating the grain from the chaff.
- He knows when I sit and when I rise.
- He knows my comings and goings.
- He is familiar with all my ways and all the words on my tongue.
- And the climax—he hems me in, behind and before.

David's summary is, "Such knowledge is too wonderful for me" (v. 6). How do you feel after reading this? Is God too close? Too intimate? I do not always like being hemmed in. So often I want my will, my way, my thoughts, only to find that God will not let me go. So often God wants more and I want less.

In verses 7–10, it might appear that David is trying to get away from God. But verses 11–12 give a different perspective. When I face the darkness of depression, discouragement, and defeat, I could easily sink under the load. But even there God's hand guides me and his right hand holds me fast.

So far David has gone from east to west, from heaven to the grave, even into unexplained darkness. Now David goes even further, back to before I was born. I can read God's thoughts about me at that time in verses 13–16.

There was never a time when I was unknown to God, never a minute when I was beyond his observation. When David writes, "My frame was not hidden from you" (v. 15), the words are a powerful reminder of the value God sets on us even in our mother's womb. "God will not leave the work of his own hands either to chance or to ultimate extinction."[3] He shaped my body, my personality and my heritage.

Psalm 119:73 says, "Your hands have made and fashioned me; give me understanding that I may learn your commandments." In the midst of his trials Job said, "Your hands shaped me and made me. Will you now turn and destroy me? Remember that you molded me like clay" (Job 10:8–9 NIV).

The prophet Jeremiah sums it up: "I know, O LORD, that the way of man is not in himself, that it is not in man who walks to direct his steps" (10:23). In chapter 18, Jeremiah visited a potter's house and saw him working at the wheel. The clay vessel he was shaping was marred in his hands, so the potter formed it into a shape that pleased him.

I too am marred clay, and God uses the difficult circumstances, the trials and hardships, to reshape me into the image of his Son. My tendency is to define my life by what I need outwardly, but God defines what I need inwardly.

The kind of searching that David describes in Psalm 139 is also written about in Hebrews 4:12–13: "The word of God is living and active, sharper than any two-edged sword, piercing to the division of soul and of spirit, of joints and of marrow, and discerning the thoughts and intentions of the heart. And no creature is hidden from his sight, but all are naked and exposed to the eyes of him to whom we must give account." God's searching of my heart is so deep that it penetrates even to the dividing of the soul and spirit. The Word not only searches, it also judges the thoughts and attitudes of my heart. Nothing is hidden from God, and it is to this God that I must give an account of my life. But notice how he wants us to approach him in Hebrews 4:14–16: "Since then we have a great high priest who has passed through the heavens, Jesus, the Son of God, let us hold fast our confession. For we do not have a high priest who is unable to sympathize with our weaknesses, but one who in every respect has been tempted as we are, yet without sin. Let us then with confidence draw near to the throne of grace, that we may receive mercy and find grace to help in time of need."

It is not always easy to submit to the searching process, especially when I uncover rebellion, unbelief, anger, and selfishness. It can be overwhelming. But I have Jesus as my Great High Priest, who cried out on the cross, "It is finished!" Because of his death, resurrection, and ascension, I now have all the rights and privileges of a child of God.

Despite living many years before this took place, David had an understanding of the deliverance from sin and oppression that God would someday bring. No wonder that at the end of Psalm 139 David cries, "Search me, O God, and know my heart! Try me and know my thoughts! And see if there be any grievous way in me, and lead me in the way everlasting" (vv. 23–24). Like David, I am not left alone to figure out the ways of God—or even the ways of my own heart. Left to myself, I would have destroyed everything I touched. But I am to remember that I am not an orphan; I am never left alone. Nothing will ever separate me from God's love, "neither death nor life, nor angels nor rulers, nor things present nor things to come, nor powers, nor height nor depth, nor anything else in all creation, will be able to separate us from the love of God in Christ Jesus our Lord" (Romans 8:38–39).

These are some of the psalms God has used to teach me about himself, his way, his thoughts, and his plans. There are many more. I encourage you to choose a particular psalm to meditate on and make it "words to live by." As Psalm 1 promises, "Blessed is the man . . . [whose] delight is in the law of the LORD, and on his law he meditates day and night" (vv. 1–2). May your prayers be blessed in that way.

15

Praying Like a Child

—⟋

When God came to conquer the kingdom of this world, he came in a way that was totally unexpected: as a baby. As Jesus grew to maturity, he turned the kingdom of this world upside down with his life, his teaching, his miracles, his death, his resurrection. I've learned that the prayers of his kingdom operate in much the same way. They start with helplessness, with a childlike faith, and end with power.

To pray for God's kingdom to come, I must come like a child. I need to become more like my sister, Barbara, who learned how to come to Jesus with childlike faith and requests large and small. In the last years of her life, Barbara's room became a place of prayer. My family and I could come to her with any request. "Barbara, I have lost my keys. Please pray that I will find them." "Barbara, my heart is distant from Jesus. Please pray for me." And so it went.

My daughter Barb or I would pray with Barbara every night

before she went to bed. My sister never forgot the people who needed prayer. She had a long list of nieces and nephews to pray for. She prayed for a young wife to become pregnant. God answered her prayer, and now I have a delightful great-granddaughter.

She prayed against the Evil One. I can still hear her prayer: "Jesus, we don't like him. He is evil. Send him away."

She loved the movie *The Parent Trap* with Lindsay Lohan. When I told her that Lindsay was in trouble, she prayed right away for her. In her later years, she was in so much pain that friends and family would come and pray with her. She would not let them leave until she prayed for them too.

Barbara was afraid of dying, so I prayed she would look forward to heaven. I prayed she would be a blessing in our home. Several times when we had to put her in a nursing home while the family was gone, I prayed that she would bless the staff. And she did. They loved having her.

During the last week of her life, she was in so much pain that we had to put her in the nursing home again. By this time she was so weak that she couldn't enjoy being there as she had before. Three days later, with her family around her singing her favorite songs, she was unaware that she was dying. In the late afternoon God quietly took her. God had answered our prayers.

Her memorial service was remarkable in that young and old came to pay tribute to her as a person who loved them. She was no respecter of persons. In the church nursery school where she participated for a few years, the young children who felt left out would come and sit on her lap. She welcomed them all as her children. We miss her.

I long for that kind of simplicity in prayer, the strong confidence that God listens. I know that my prayers and my sister's prayers are in "golden bowls full of incense, which are the prayers of the saints" (Revelation 5:8). And I know that my prayers have been helped by the things I have learned, in part, from my sister.

I am learning that life is a battle. The Enemy is relentless. He will do everything in his power to divert me from a simple and pure devotion to Christ. Without prayer, I will drift.

I am learning that fruitful ministry comes out of weakness, not perceived strength. It is the ministry of the Spirit. I am totally dependent on him.

I am learning that I am never through with sin. Old sinful habits and patterns of thinking and living will surface and need to be radically dealt with. I must always go to Christ, trusting in his blood, keeping a good conscience and a lifestyle of forgiveness.

I am learning about the absolute supremacy of Christ in ruling the nations. I am learning that I am a partner in his kingdom moving forward.

I am learning to leave behind theological language and to be much more interactive in my teaching. I continue to learn that truth must first speak to my heart before I can share it with others.

I am learning I need to turn away daily from selfish thoughts and desires and to let the Spirit teach me how to love.

God is a missionary God. I am no longer content with a life that does not have a kingdom perspective. I am absolutely convinced that his kingdom moves forward against the kingdom of darkness by the simple, powerful prayers of a childlike faith.

The God of the Impossible

On our first trip to Uganda, Jack and I stayed in a hotel in Kampala with many Asians who had survived the years under Amin. It wasn't long before we were accepted by Hindus from India and Muslims from Pakistan. God used those experiences to help Jack see that the "nations"—particularly those from Asian cultures—had come to England. The result was that WHM began a work in the Southall area of London where many Asians live. In 1994 my daughter Keren, her husband Bob Heppe, and their four children moved to London to bring the gospel to Hindus, Sikhs, and Muslims.

A few years after Jack died, I sensed God's call to join them. Many of the Asians come from Kenya and Uganda, fleeing persecution. My heart is stirred by the sorrows and heartaches of their lives. Over the years I have also listened to Bob talk about God's passion to reach the nations as he sends us with good news into a world broken by sin. I am not here for myself!

So, when I was invited to India to speak at a conference, it seemed natural to say yes. Two prayer partners came with me, Jane Wills from Spain and my friend Saroj from London. It was a truly blessed time. I loved being in India. I loved the people and I loved seeing what God was doing. Bob was with us too as we came to do a Sonship week with young men and women who were being trained to be pastors and teachers.

In London, we have four charity shops where we sell Punjabi suits and saris, books, and household goods. In India there is a Christian organization that teaches rag pickers to make bags, scarves, greeting cards, and shawls. Bob buys what the ladies make to sell in our shops. While we were in India, it was a joy for me to visit some of their children in their very simple school. We also visited some of the mothers in the one-room homes they share with their children. It was a joy to see what God was doing.

The next year when another invitation came, I was eager to return. This time Kathy Hall came as my prayer partner. Gloria Shaw, the organizer, put together a one-day event for about ninety women. We gathered for tea, a special meal and four talks about women from the Bible who were just like us, though they lived many years ago. It was moving to stand before these ladies and talk about the God for whom nothing is impossible. Ruth Batstone spoke about Eve, I spoke on Sarah and Hannah, and an Asian woman did a study on Mary.

The theme of our talks was "Nothing Is Impossible with God." I chose the four women: Eve, Sarah, Hannah, and Mary, and interacted with the other speakers about the themes of their lives. Their stories are included in this section. Let me share why I chose these particular women.

Eve believed an impossible lie. In my life journey, I have realized that if I had been in the garden of Eden, I too would have chosen to eat the fruit rather than submit to God. The impossible lie that beguiled Eve was that God was withholding something from her. Satan knew how to seduce her and twist God's word to his advantage: "Did God really say?" (Genesis 3:1 NIV). We need to know what God really said and we need to listen when he speaks. We especially need to listen when he says, "I will never leave you nor forsake you" (Hebrews 13:5).

Sarah believed an impossible promise. Sarah was asked to believe God's promise that she would have a son. Her problem was that she had been barren—infertile—for many years. This was a very important promise. God had told her husband Abraham that he would be the father of nations, so it was crucial for both Abraham and Sarah to believe that God would do the impossible. What did I learn from Sarah? I like to take matters into my own hands like Sarah did. I am impatient in waiting for God to work out his plans. Like Sarah, I need the laughter of faith for the impossibilities of life. Sarah's laugh was a genuine laugh of faith when, at ninety years of age, she held little Isaac in her arms.

Hannah prayed an impossible prayer. We hear Hannah praying twice: once in desperation and once in faith regarding who God is and what he is doing in her life and in the nations. I was captured by her plea, "If you will only . . . give [me] a son" (1 Samuel 1:11 NIV). It reminded me of prayers I have prayed: "If only you had not taken Jack, I would not be so lonely." It is too easy to live out of the "if onlys" of life and not come to the place of faith as Hannah did. God answered her prayer and gave her a son, whom God used to bring his people back to himself. Jesus' mother Mary recited Hannah's second prayer to her cousin Elizabeth after she found out she was pregnant with Jesus. I longed to be able to exalt God in prayer the way she did.

Mary was given an impossible task: giving birth to the Son of

God and nurturing him into manhood. She humbly submitted to God's plan for her life and brought forth the One who would save his people from their sins. But there was another side to Mary. She also needed a Savior, and I wonder if it all came together for her when she saw her son die that she might live. Scripture's last mention of her has her praying in the upper room, waiting for the coming of the Spirit—the One Jesus promised while he was here on earth. Like Mary, God also has given me a task: bearing children, taking people into our home, going to places like Uganda, London, and India. Like Mary, I too am flawed, but I have the same Savior she did. She is truly a blessed woman, and I am blessed too.

16

Eve Believed an Impossible Lie

⌐‿

Everywhere I go in the world, women tell me about their fears. In the United States, we live in a climate of fear. We talk about our fear with one another; we feed it with our TV viewing and news reading. When our working theology or philosophy is fear, what follows is guilt, depression, and a lifestyle comprised of complaining, blame shifting, and defensiveness.

There is fear

of the future,

that we will fail in our parenting,

that our marriages won't last,

of death,

of suffering,

of failure,

of people's opinions,

of losing control, and

of the unknown.

Parents are afraid of their children's opinions and children afraid of their parents' opinions. Single parents are afraid of how their children are affected by divorce, and the list goes on.

What is the source of our fear?

OUR MOTHER, EVE

About thirty-five years ago, I asked myself, "Who am I? Why am I filled with fear and guilt?" On the surface I knew I was a wife and mother and someone involved in ministry, but I really didn't know who the real Rose Marie was. So I took my Bible and studied my first mother, Eve, in Genesis, chapters 1 through 3.

Eve is the only woman who ever lived who had no history of sin. She didn't have a clue as to what it would look like. She had a perfect husband, a beautiful place to live, and an unmarred relationship with God. Yet, it wasn't enough for her. The Lord's provision for Eve and her husband, Adam, is a model of parental care. They are sheltered but not smothered. Isn't that what we would all want today—a sense of God's parental care, a perfect husband, a life of peace, and an ideal environment? However, there was only one thing Eve could not have. That was the fruit from the Tree of the Knowledge of Good and Evil, which stood in the middle of the garden of Eden. God had said that if Adam and Eve ate the fruit of that tree, they would die.

Satan came to the garden to tempt Eve to do that very thing. He said she wouldn't die, but that in reality she would be like God, knowing good and evil. Eve listened. She looked at the fruit and saw that it was good for food. She thought about how it would make her wise if she ate it. In her reply to Satan she said, "God said we must not eat of the tree or touch it" (Genesis 3:3, paraphrased). But God had never said it shouldn't be touched; only that it couldn't be eaten. Eve did not want to submit to God who denied her the one thing she thought she had the right to, to be like God, to be in control. What a heady thought! That's why Satan's temptation appealed to her.

As I thought about Eve, I realized that if I had been there, I would have eaten the fruit just as she had. I would not have wanted God to deny me anything. As Derek Kidner observes, "The pattern of sin runs right through the act, for Eve listened to a creature instead of the Creator, followed her impressions against her instructions, and made self-fulfillment her goal."[1] From that act of disobedience—as she followed her impressions over her instructions—our first mother became afraid and ashamed. Fear, blame shifting, pain in childbirth, hard labor for Adam, and expulsion from the garden were now before them. And later on, the impact of sin was played out in the lives of her sons Cain and Abel. Can you imagine how Eve felt when she lost her first two sons: Cain killing Abel and subsequently banished to a life of wandering?

What I learned about Eve I also see in myself: I love control and I am a rebel at heart. Control promises so much! It feeds pride and arrogance when what you do works, but it brings despair and fear when you sense that life is out of control. I learned this well growing up. My mother was a suicidal paranoid schizophrenic. My father and I kept a constant, watchful eye to keep her from hurting herself. It "worked" in the sense that she lived to be 104 years old. But the illusion was that it was our efforts that kept her alive. My father and I paid a big price in fear, isolation, and loneliness. My coping strategy was to build emotional walls to isolate myself from my mother and from God. First, it was as if my walls were walls of cloth, then wood, then iron. When they became iron walls of self-protection, only God himself could pull them down.

The disobedience of Adam and Eve plunged us all into a world of suffering and the often unimaginable cruelty of one human being to another. Worst of all, we are alienated from God. No wonder we are so fearful! Sin, suffering, and death were not part of God's original created order. There was no sin and no suffering in the world before our first parents rebelled against God. But now life is full of pain and suffering, and we don't know how to handle it, so we become filled with fear.

THE SOURCE OF OUR FEARS

One source of our fear is our tendency, like Eve, to rebel against the plan and purpose of God. We are filled with fear because we don't know him well enough to trust him. In Genesis 3:21, God made garments of skin for Adam and his wife and clothed them. They were banished from the garden, and an angel with a flaming sword barred the way to the Tree of Life. Now the sinner is excluded. The way back is impossible. Adam and Eve cannot save themselves, nor can we. We have not glorified God or given him thanks. Our thinking has become futile and our foolish hearts darkened (Romans 1:21). The wisdom the Serpent promised Eve only became foolishness.

The connection between fear and my heart's inclination to rely on self, independent of God, is something I've faced many times, even after I left my parents' home. When Jack and I married, we had three goals: Jack was to finish his education, we would not use birth control, and we would live as God provided. In the first four years of our marriage God gave us four children. After twelve years, Jack completed all of his education, including a Ph.D. and a seminary degree, with no debts. We had met our goals and were very pleased about it. I sensed the hand of God on all we did—until Jack became a pastor.

At that point life spun out of control. Jack's salary didn't meet our needs, and the church work was difficult, absorbing much of his time and attention. This was not what I had planned. The walls I had first built when caring for my mother went up a little higher this time. Four years later, our family moved to Philadelphia and Jack began to teach at Westminster Seminary. God did a deep work of repentance and faith in my husband during that time, and many young people were drawn to his preaching and teaching. Troubled young men and women found their way to our church and our home. It was not uncommon to have every bed filled with confused but searching young people. But at the height of all this blessing, our daughter Barbara walked out of our lives. She did not want anything more to do with us—or with God.

New fears surfaced. How could this happen? We had trained, taught, nurtured, and loved our children and they seemed to be doing well in every way. But now our family was out of control, and my emotions were too. Anger, fear, resentment, and bitterness gripped my heart and mind. I did not know how to fix this; I had no answers. In the midst of all this, my husband was teaching the young leaders of our church the basics of the gospel. During one talk, he gave an illustration about Martin Luther and Erasmus arguing the nature of grace. Erasmus likened grace to a parent helping a toddler cross the room to get a gift from the other parent. He was saying that grace assisted our strength. Martin Luther said "No, no! Grace is what reaches down to rescue a caterpillar surrounded by a ring of fire." I knew I was that caterpillar in a ring of fire. I was helpless. I couldn't save my daughter; I couldn't love people; and most of all I couldn't help myself. I had to cry, "Who shall deliver me from all my fears and the shame and guilt that come with them?" I needed a deliverance from above that had nothing to do with control or performance, and this is what Jesus gave me.

During a trip to Switzerland God showed me how I had mis-handled my life, trying to live independently of him and do everything in my own strength. He broke me of my stubborn, fearful, rebellious independence, and I felt the kiss of his forgive-ness. Now, instead of my proud and fearful autonomy, I had the joy, the freedom, and the assurance of being a daughter of God. Eve and her husband Adam had gone their own way in the gar-den, rebelling against their Creator. But Jesus, the second Adam, lived the perfect life that Adam, Eve, and I had failed to live. Then he died on the cross to pay the penalty for my sins and give me his righteousness instead (2 Corinthians 5:21).

When we see Jesus suffering on the cross to pay for *our* sins and bring us back to God, we have a new way to understand the suffering of this world and our fears about it. We see that God cares about us and all the suffering Eve and Adam's sin caused. In fact, he cared enough to experience it with us. Alister McGrath writes, "The cross of Christ stands as a solemn and powerful reminder that God himself was prepared to suffer in order to redeem his people. [God] *is* pained by the suffering of the world. His very nature leads him to decide that he will enter into it, as one of us, in the person of his Son, Jesus Christ. In his love for us, he bears our sorrows and is acquainted with our grief. God allowed himself to be hurt by the suffering of the world."[2]

If God has done all this, why do we continue to be so fearful? How can we deal with our fears? My daughter Barbara now has four children. (The story of her return to the Lord is in the book she wrote with her father, *Come Back, Barbara*.) Barbara's second son, Gabriel, has neurofibromatosis, a disease in which tumors grow on nerve endings throughout his body. It is difficult to operate on the tumors because they are entangled with the nerves. It is a painful and unpredictable disease. Barbara once wrote a poem about her fears for Gabe.

> My Tiger and Faith
>
> I like to keep my tiger in a cage.
> It's not tame, you know,
> only contained.
> I like to keep my tiger all tied up
> Then close the door
> and walk away.
> I'd like to keep that tiger far away
> But when it gets fresh meat—
> A new fear or worry to gnaw—
> It begins to roar and pace.
> I like to keep my tiger in that cage
> But sometimes it escapes
> Fills my mind and heart with fear
> And forces me to live by faith.[3]

At one point, Gabriel was on interferon for nine months, and it made him very sick. Many people prayed for him, and then Gabe prayed that God would stop the growth of the tumors. The next MRI showed that the tumors had not grown, which was an encouragement to everyone's faith. Whatever lies ahead for Gabe, the suffering in his life and in Barbara's forces her to live by faith, to fix her eyes on Jesus. She needs faith that God has a good, sovereign, wise plan for Gabe and the rest of her family.

FIX YOUR EYES ON JESUS

Our basic problem is this: *We don't trust the plan.* We are taught by our flesh, by Satan, by our culture, even by other Christians, that we must do everything we can to avoid suffering. "Save yourself!" is the cry of our culture. But that is just what Jesus refused to do, even when those crucifying him said, "You saved others—now save yourself!" (Luke 23:35 paraphrased). He endured unfathomable suffering to the end to secure our salvation and defeat the things we need to fear the most.

"Fix [your] eyes on Jesus" (Hebrews 12:2, NIV) is the battle cry during suffering. But how do you do this when you have a son with an incurable disease? Where is faith in a loving God when you are paralyzed from the neck down from a diving accident like Joni Eareckson Tada? When you read Joni's books, you sometimes forget that she can't walk, write, take a bath, brush her hair, or do many of the things we take for granted. She has learned painfully, with much struggle, to rest in the all-wise God whose love for her included not only the redemption of her soul but strength and courage to draw upon the sufficiency of God's grace each day.

My friend Sue Cortese has three children with autism. Her husband also struggles with this disorder, and they are guardians of a young girl whose mother was a drug addict. She writes,

There will be no lasting peace unless I realize that life is carefully crafted by the Lover of my soul, who didn't give me heaven as a place to live but *himself.* This really is a broken world, isn't it? It seems a bad enough place to need a very powerful Savior. Things don't get fixed—utopia doesn't come through human will power and ingenuity. Suffering goes on and on and on. This world will never be heaven. But as long as Jesus is present in our sufferings—and his purposes are being accomplished even if it looks as hopeless and pointless as the cross did to his disciples—then life in this dying world still tastes of the heaven to come.

We both agreed that we see through a glass darkly. But we, like Barbara, fix our eyes on Jesus, the author and finisher of our faith.

There are two kingdoms at war in this world: the kingdom of light and the kingdom of darkness. Satan, the Father of Lies, seeks to keep us from fixing our eyes on Jesus. Like Eve, we can still be vulnerable to his lies. We must recognize them for what they are and close our ears and hearts to them. Satan will always try to get us to focus our attention on ourselves or our circumstances and then leave us without hope. I think of the struggles I often had in Uganda to love and serve the people there. I struggled because I believed Satan's lie that God would not help me love; therefore, I was on my own.

Paul writes to the Corinthians, "But I am afraid that just as Eve was deceived by the serpent's cunning, your minds may some-how be led astray from your sincere and pure devotion to Christ" (2 Corinthians 11:3 NIV). Paul's fear was that these believers would not be devoted to Christ. This was a genuine fear, one we should take seriously as well.

What do we do with our fears? Listen to what God says through Paul. We were "in slavery [to fear] . . . but when the time had fully come, God sent his Son, born of a woman, born under law, to redeem those under law, that we might receive the full rights of sons. Because you are sons, God sent the Spirit of his Son into our hearts, the Spirit who calls out, 'Abba, Father.' So you are no longer a slave, but a son; and since you are a son, God has made you also an heir" (Galatians 4:3–7 NIV).

You no longer live under a system of do's and don'ts, rules and regulations. Christ kept the law fully for you, the law you could never keep. Now God has sent the Spirit of his Son into our hearts. In your loneliness, in your suffering, in your fears, the cry of the heart is the "Abba Father" cry. You do not need to act like a spiritual orphan, as Jack once challenged me. God's promise is that you are not alone to figure out your life. The Holy Spirit listens to the Father and prays for us according to the Father's will. So trust the Son! Trust the Holy Spirit!

Eve lived independently, on her own terms, as a rebel. Her daughters, like me, follow her in that autonomy, and we also know what it is like to live alone in fear, as orphans. But there is another way of being alone. In John 12 the Greeks came to see Jesus. Their visit signaled to Jesus that it is now time for him to die. He says, "I tell you the truth, unless a kernel of wheat falls to the ground and dies, it remains only a single seed [or "alone"]. But if it dies, it produces many seeds. The man who loves his life will lose it, while the man who hates his life in this world will keep it for eternal life" (John 12:24–25 NIV). This is a call to die to self to follow Christ so that you do not remain a single seed, alone.

This last year in London, I was sick. I am still living out of a suitcase and doing a lot of traveling. At Easter time I was overwhelmed by missing my husband, who died on Easter Monday. One day the Spirit spoke to my heart through this passage of the seed dying. I knew I would be "a seed alone" if I didn't die to my expectations, desires, longings, and plans. This kind of dying goes on each day. But when the seed dies, it brings forth fruit. The fruit of peace, joy, love and patience is worth waiting for. When we accept God's plans, even though they seem to be veiled in mystery, the fruit is a quiet and gentle spirit, God's gift to those who truly fix their eyes on Jesus.

17

Sarah Believed an Impossible Promise

⟜⟋

E ventually the outworking of sin that started with Adam and
Eve became so bad that God was ready to wipe out all the
people of the earth. But God is the God with whom all things are
possible. A man named Noah found favor with God, and God
commanded him to build an ark to save his family and the animals of the earth.

GOD'S IMPOSSIBLE PROMISE

God could not wipe out the human race because he had made a
promise that had to be kept. It was the promise he made to Adam
and Eve that their sin and disobedience were not the end of the
story. God promised that a Deliverer would come to crush the
head of the Enemy (Genesis 3:15).

Through Noah's line, Abraham was born. Now God was ready to put his plan into action. When Abraham was seventy-five years old and his wife Sarah was sixty-five, God told them to leave their home in Ur, a city located in present-day Turkey, and go and settle in Palestine.

What must Sarah have thought when she was told they were to leave the place of her birth, her family, and all the comforts of a big city to move to a desolate land where she would live in tents the rest of her life.

One thing surely must have sounded good to her. At sixty-five years of age, Sarah had no children, but she knew the promise God gave to Abraham: "I will make you into a great nation and I will bless you; I will make your name great, and you will be a blessing. I will bless those who bless you, and whoever curses you I will curse; and all peoples on earth will be blessed through you" (Genesis 12:2–3 NIV).

That sounded good to Sarah. Of course the blessings would include her. She liked the idea of greatness: big family, great nation, great name. Imagine all the peoples of the earth being blessed through her and Abraham!

But time passed, and no child came. And then there was a side trip to Egypt because of a famine in the land. Here Abraham tells Sarah, "I know that you are a woman beautiful in appearance, and when the Egyptians see you, they will say, 'This is his wife.' Then they will kill me, but they will let you live. Say you are my sister, that it may go well with me because of you, and that my life may be spared for your sake" (Genesis 12:11–13).

Sarah did what Abraham asked, but how do you think she felt? If she were taken as Pharaoh's wife, what about the promise of God? Maybe she thought greatness would come through Pharaoh.

But the larger question is, "What is God going to do to protect Sarah and his promise?" Because he did protect her: "The LORD afflicted Pharaoh and his house with great plagues because of [Sarah], [Abraham's] wife" (Genesis 12:17). Soon she was returned to her husband along with many gifts.

God protected Sarah, and he also protected his promise that through her, Abraham would have a son. Pharaoh sent the couple home, back to Bethel. There Abraham called on the name of the Lord. He hadn't done that before they went to Egypt. Now the relationship with God is re-established.

SARAH'S SOLUTION—BUT NOT GOD'S

Ten years have passed since Abraham and Sarah first came into the land, and they have no children. She is now seventy-five years old. Maybe it is still possible, but time is moving on. Sarah now takes charge. She believed the promise, but there had to be a practical way to get things moving!

Abraham and Sarah had brought a maidservant home with them from Egypt. Sarah says to Abraham, "The LORD has kept me from having children. Go, sleep with my maidservant; perhaps I can build a family through her" (Genesis 16:2 NIV).

God's promise had been very specific. God was going to bless the world through Abraham *and Sarah*. The detour into Egypt was not God's plan; neither was it God's plan to build a family in the way Sarah proposed. In the culture in which they lived, it was acceptable to raise a family using other women. But this was not what God had said.

To wait for the fulfillment of God's promise is not easy, especially if you start to wonder if it is really going to happen. Eve did not follow her instructions, and Sarah could not wait. In both cases the consequences were disastrous.

Abraham listened to his wife, slept with Hagar, and she conceived. A son is born, but not the son God had promised.

Now Hagar takes the upper hand and treats Sarah with contempt. Sarah blames Abraham and asks God to judge between the two of them. Like Adam and Eve, who shifted the blame when they disobeyed God, Abraham dismisses the whole thing and tells Sarah to do what she wants. Sarah deals harshly with Hagar, and Hagar runs away. Notice the pattern of sin:

1. God gave a specific promise: Sarah and Abraham would have a son.
2. Time passes; they become older and there is still no child.
3. Sarah takes matters into her own hands.
4. When her plans go awry, she mistreats her handmaiden.
5. Sarah blames the whole thing on Abraham.

In the New Testament, James, a brother of our Lord Jesus writes: "When tempted, no one should say, 'God is tempting me.' For God cannot be tempted by evil . . . but each one is tempted when, by his own evil desire, he is dragged away and enticed. Then, after desire has conceived, it gives birth to sin; and sin, when it is full-grown, gives birth to death" (James 1:13–15 NIV).

Eve was persuaded to sin by the serpent. Sarah thought to solve her problem by doing what the culture said was acceptable. In both cases we see that sin has consequences. Yet, as evil as our actions are, they never abort God's plan to fulfill his promises.

My husband and I had four children in four years. I believed I was building a family for God. So I trained, disciplined, taught the Bible, taught manners, and gave my children rules to follow. Twenty-one years later, when the youngest of the four rebelled and left home angry and bitter, eventually living with drug dealers, I realized that much of what I had done was motivated by wanting a perfect family that did not embarrass me. Her younger sister, our fifth child, was influenced by her and also went her own way. It was a very sad and humbling time. I had missed the fact that only God changes the heart. I was expecting all my work to do what only God can do.

God builds his family by leading us to trust him. Yes, we guide and instruct but always with grace and love, recognizing that we too need grace and mercy each day. Psalm 127 is a special guide to mothers. It begins: "Unless the LORD builds the house, those who build it labor in vain" (Psalm 127:1). This psalm reminds us that God alone builds the house. You don't have to lose even one night's sleep because your children belong to God. He will make them warriors in the kingdom.

GOD'S IMPOSSIBLE PROMISE FULFILLED

God meets Hagar in the wilderness and tells her to return home. Sarah has to live in the same household with Hagar and her son for another fifteen years. It could not have been easy for her.

When Abraham is ninety-nine years old and Sarah eighty-nine, God tells Abraham, "I will bless [Sarah] and will surely give you a son by her. I will bless her so that she will be the mother of nations; kings of peoples will come from her" (Genesis 17:15–16 NIV).

Abraham pleads with God to let Hagar's son Ishmael be the heir, the promised son. God says No. God is not through with Sarah.

One day three men visit Abraham. Water is set out to wash their feet, and a lavish meal is prepared. They eat while Abraham stands by. One of them asks, "Where is your wife Sarah?"

Abraham replies, "There, in the tent." And now we know that one of the men is the LORD for he says, "I will surely return to you about this time next year, and Sarah your wife will have a son" (Genesis 18:9–10 NIV).

Sarah, listening, "laughed to herself as she thought, 'After I am worn out and my master is old, will I now have this pleasure?' Then the LORD said to Abraham, 'Why did Sarah laugh and say, "Will I really have a child, now that I am old?" Is anything too hard for the LORD? I will return to you at the appointed time next year and Sarah will have a son'" (vv. 12–14 NIV).

Is anything too hard for the Lord? This phrase echoes through the Bible. We will hear it again when the angel speaks to Mary, "Nothing is impossible with God" (Luke 1:37 NIV).

God was dealing with the problem Sarah had had all along. She could not wait; she did not believe the promise and took matters into her own hands. God needs to deal with the basic problems of her life and ours: Unbelief—lack of faith—and the fear that comes when somehow we need to make things happen. This was also Eve's problem. God could not be trusted. She had to take matters into her own hands, trusting her impressions and not her instructions.

But one year later Isaac was born—at the very time God had promised. "By faith Sarah herself received power to conceive, even when she was past the age, since she considered him faithful who had promised" (Hebrews 11:11). And Sarah laughs again. This time it is the laughter of pure joy.

WE ARE DAUGHTERS OF SARAH

Sarah received strength to conceive because she considered God faithful to keep his promises. Two thousand years later, a disciple of Jesus reflected on the life of Sarah and wrote, "Your beauty should not come from outward adornment, such as braided hair and the wearing of gold jewelry and fine clothes. Instead, it should be that of your inner self, the unfading beauty of a gentle and quiet spirit, which is of great worth in God's sight" (1 Peter 3:3–4 NIV). He later adds, "You are [Sarah's] daughters if you do what is right and do not give way to fear" (v. 6).

Sarah learned that there were no "second causes." God was the one who closed her womb for twenty-five years. He was the one who protected her in Egypt. He was the one who protected her when Abraham took her into a desert kingdom and asked her again to protect him by saying she was his sister. He is the one who graciously uncovered her unbelief, and then gave her the joy of her life a year later. Sarah lived until she was 127 years old, long enough to watch her son grow into manhood.

There are more lessons to be learned from Sarah. There are layers of lessons to be learned from God's initial promise, to the fulfillment of the promise, to how it affects our lives. It is the story of grace.

Building a family through Hagar was the product of Sarah's self-effort—of trying to accomplish God's will in her own strength. Hagar's son was born in the ordinary way; Isaac was the son of promise, born in an extraordinary way. In the letter to the Galatians, Paul writes that Isaac was born by the power of the Spirit. We too are born by the power of the Spirit, by faith in the Son of God who loved us and gave himself for us (Galatians 2:20). We are not slaves; we are free, free to please God, free to trust, and free to live by the Spirit's power and not our own strength (Galatians 4:28–31 paraphrased).

The promise to Adam and Eve has been kept. Christ in his death and resurrection crushed the head of the Serpent, Satan, at the cross, disarming him. The promise to Abraham and Sarah has been kept. Abraham is still the father of nations. We are all proof of that.

We are not slaves. In all the hard circumstances of our lives we serve God for whom all things are possible. We are free to live out of his resources and not our own. Learn from Sarah not to give way to fear but to trust God to fulfill his purpose and will for our lives.

18

Hannah Prayed an Impossible Prayer

⌒

In C. S. Lewis' book, *The Lion, the Witch and the Wardrobe*, four children arrive in Narnia, a magical country under the spell of the White Witch. Aslan, the king of Narnia, is nowhere to be found, but rumor has it that he is "on the move." He appears to have abandoned his kingdom to the White Witch, who spends her time turning its inhabitants into statues. The children meet Mr. and Mrs. Beaver, who assure them that Aslan will return and set things right. A prophecy even suggests that they will have a central part in the drama that is about to unfold. They learn they are to rule with Aslan in the royal city.

Faced with this exciting news, Lucy and Susan, two of the children, wonder what Aslan is like.

"Is—is he a man?" asked Lucy. "Aslan, a man!" said Mr. Beaver sternly. "Certainly not! I tell you he is the King of the wood and the son of the great Emperor-Beyond-the-Sea. Don't you know who is the King of Beasts? Aslan is a lion—*the* Lion, the great Lion."

"Ooh!" said Susan, "I'd thought he was a man. Is he—quite safe? I shall feel rather nervous about meeting a lion."

"That you will, dearie, and no mistake," said Mrs. Beaver, "if there's anyone who can appear before Aslan without their knees knocking, they're either braver than most or else just silly."

"Then he isn't safe?" said Lucy.

"Safe?" said Mr. Beaver. "Don't you hear what Mrs. Beaver tells you? Who said anything about safe? 'Course he isn't safe. But he's good. He's the King, I tell you."[1]

Like Narnia under the control of the White Witch, God's children at the time when the judges ruled were in desperate need of a deliverer. In the book of Judges we read this lament, "O LORD, the God of Israel, why has this happened in Israel, that today there should be one tribe lacking in Israel?" (Judges 21:3). The book ends with this verse: "In those days there was no king in Israel. Everyone did what was right in his own eyes" (21:25). This is a sad lament in light of the promise in Deuteronomy 17:25 that God would give them a king when they came into the land. It seemed as if God had forsaken his people.

A woman named Hannah lived during this time in Israel's history. She too must have felt that God had forsaken her. Yet God would use her suffering to bring his people the king he promised. Just as the children in Narnia found out that Aslan was good, so God's people were going to find out that God is also good.

HANNAH SUFFERS GOD'S DELAY

First Samuel 1 opens with the story of a family. Elkanah had two wives, Hannah and Peninnah. Peninnah had children, but

Hannah had none. This family faithfully went to Shiloh year after year to worship and sacrifice to the LORD Almighty. When the day came for his sacrifice, Elkanah would give portions of the meat to Peninnah and to all her sons and daughters. But to Hannah he gave a double portion because he loved her, despite the fact that the Lord had closed Hannah's womb, making her infertile (1 Samuel 1:5). Because of this, her rival Peninnah kept provoking her to irritate her. This went on year after year.

Hannah had to endure Peninnah's accusations and her own sense of worthlessness because she had no children. And since Elkanah loved Hannah more than Peninnah, this added to Peninnah's bitterness. We don't know how long this went on, but year after year may have been a long time. Hannah must have felt that God had abandoned her. To have children in the Jewish culture was an evident sign of God's blessing. To have none was seen as a sign that God was displeased. Elkanah said to her, "Why do you weep? And why do you not eat? And why is your heart sad? Am I not more to you than ten sons?" (1 Samuel 1:8). Even the love of her husband wasn't enough for Hannah.

Finally, on one of the trips to the temple, Hannah hit bottom. She couldn't eat and couldn't seem to stop crying. Weeping bitterly, she went to the temple and prayed to the Lord. She went to the only one who could solve her problem and vowed, "O LORD Almighty, if you will only look upon your servant's misery and remember me, and not forget your servant but give her a son, then I will give him to the LORD for all the days of his life, and no razor will ever be used on his head." (1 Samuel 1:11–12 NIV).

In her prayer Hannah was saying, God has kept me from having children and he is the only one who can give me a son. God was the first cause. Her need was to pray and live in his presence with the knowledge that God had sovereignly closed her womb. If he would only look upon her in her distress and give her a son, she would give him back to the Lord all the days of his life.

What does it mean to live in God's presence? Start by believing that God's plans are good and that the kingdom of God is coming through the crises of your life. You cannot rest in God's presence when you have judged and rejected God's plan. As you face the difficult circumstances of your life, does it seem impossible to you that God has a good plan for you that includes the expansion of his kingdom? If we don't see God as the first cause of the events in our lives, we will complain, excuse ourselves, and blame others because we didn't get what we thought we deserved. We will get angry because of the way we were treated or spend a lot of energy proving to ourselves and others that we are right. Having done my share of all these things, I've had to learn to believe that God is good and in sovereign control of every circumstance of my life. This was not an easy lesson to learn, but it is where I have always had to start, especially since the death of my husband Jack in 1996.

A year after Jack died, I was in Spain with two of my children and their families, the Heppes and the Julianis. In that beautiful place where the mountains came down to the blue-green sea, surrounded by the love and care of my family, I still felt intensely alone. One evening, the words "If only" kept coming to my mind. I remembered the words of Hannah in her agony. If only Jack hadn't died, I wouldn't feel so lonely and unsettled. Jack and I had come to Spain for sixteen years, and I longed for the past.

A few days later, I mentioned this to my son-in-law Angelo and he said, "You are looking to the past with nostalgia and romanticizing the future." I was hoping that someone would come into my life to ease the pain of loneliness. There was also an element of fear as I looked to the future. Would God be enough? Would he truly love and care for me as he had in the past? I discovered that there were two doors I had to close. One door was longing for the past and the other was fantasizing about the future. Angelo prayed for me, and I brought my loneliness to God. He gave me his peace, and I was then free to enjoy the time with my family, at peace in a place that held so many good memories for me. It is not easy to deal with God as the first cause. I have to keep bringing the loneliness and the longings to him. But as I do so and submit to his will for me, he draws me into his presence.

GOD'S SOVEREIGNTY IN SUFFERING

My friend Betty Herron was part of New Life Church in its earliest days, and she and her husband Dan later served as missionaries to Uganda. During that time, Betty was diagnosed with cancer and after a long battle was facing her death, leaving behind her husband and five children. She wrote to me, "Accepting God as the first cause has been a sweet relief." She quoted Samuel Rutherford in her letter. This is what she learned from him.

> How hard it is to be patient if we allow our thoughts to become stuck down among the confused rolling and wheels of second causes. By this I mean all the times we say, "If only I hadn't been in the wrong place. If only I had done it differently. If only this hadn't happened to me." I mean the subtle temptation to link together earthly causes and effects. I need to fight against the temptation to accept the confused, grinding, second wheel of this logic. The answer to this is "Look up." Look to the master-motion and the first wheel. It is a petty view of our Father's love, goodness, and wisdom that

demands or expects an answer according to our desires apart from his wisdom. We see hardly one inch of the narrow land of time. To our God eternity lies open as a meadow. It must seem strange to the heavenly people, who have reached the beautiful End, that we should ever question what Love allows to be, or that we even call prayer unanswered when it is not what we expect.[2]

After reading this quote, Betty said she learned to submit to God as the first cause. He was taking her to be with him, and she was leaving her family in his care. In that crisis of faith Betty wrote,

Will God provide for and love my family? Will they keep close to him or will this drive them apart or away from God? I do have a boldness in believing that he loves me and has the best plan. This gives me a lot of daily joy, little fear, sweet relief to know there is a greater master of my life than myself, and an acceptance of negative news that we get from time to time concerning the progression of my cancer—even, amazingly, an acceptance of my inability to do much and to have to watch Dan doing everything and my not being able to help much.

A month after she wrote this letter, God took her home.

Why did God take Betty home when her heart longed to be with her family? When she had a burning desire to be a teacher of women in Uganda? Why did God take my husband? Why did God let Hannah go on year after year with a rival bitterly provoking her? Like Susan in Narnia, we sometimes think that God doesn't seem safe. What is God's purpose in sending suffering, delays, hardships, and seemingly unanswered prayer?

In his book *Why Does God Allow Suffering?* Alister McGrath writes,

> Suffering serves a vital spiritual function. It reminds us of our mortality, preventing us from entertaining delusions about our nature and our future. . . . The great prize which is set before us is none other than a relationship with God himself. But our vision is so distorted by sin that we see nothing but the lesser prizes around us. We are called by God to find our rest in him. But our hearing is so dulled that we hear only the voices of the world and its transient goals. We settle for the shadows of the grand delights for which we were created.[3]

We have been created in the image of God with the ultimate aim of finding our rest in him. The love of God is concerned with enabling us to achieve our true potential—to find peace and fulfillment with the living and loving God and to be in tune with his purposes. Suffering alone will not bring us into God's presence. Suffering with submission to the Father is what allows our relationship with him to grow deeper and sweeter.

HANNAH'S PRAYER

Why did God delay so long in giving Hannah a son? God needed to deliver his people from "everyone [doing] what was right in his own eyes" (Judges 17:6). He needed to prepare his people for a king. But first he needed a man of prayer to lead his people. And in order to have a man of prayer, he needed to raise up a woman of prayer who was able to see a kingdom that was beyond her immediate need to bear children. This is always God's way. He always has a bigger plan. It is a wise plan. It is a good plan. And we all struggle with it because we get caught up in the secondary causes.

Hannah prays to the Lord Almighty. This is the first time in the Bible that God is designated by this title. It is a reference to the sovereignty of God over all powers in the universe. God was ready to do something big for his people, and Hannah would later revel in this truth in a prayer of triumph. But Hannah's first prayer was one of desperation.

Hannah is praying for a son, vowing to give him to God for service in his kingdom. As she is praying at the temple, the priest sees her mouth moving but hears no sound. Formerly, Hannah was harassed by Peninnah; now Eli accuses her of being drunk. He said, "'How long will you keep on getting drunk? Get rid of your wine.' 'Not so my lord,' Hannah replied, 'I am a woman who is deeply troubled. I have not been drinking wine or beer; I was pouring out my soul to the LORD. Do not take your servant for a wicked woman; I have been praying here out of my great anguish and grief'" (1 Samuel 1:14–16 NIV).

Eli, moved with compassion and led by God, said, "Go in peace, and may the God of Israel grant you what you have asked of him" (1:17 NIV). Hannah accepted this as God speaking to her. She said, "'May your servant find favor in your eyes.' Then she went her way and ate something, and her face was no longer downcast" (1:18 NIV).

Something happened to Hannah when she went to the temple. This was where God dwelt with his people; the priest was God's representative on earth. Believing what God promised through the priest brought Hannah into God's presence.

Early the next morning the family returned home. Now "the LORD remembered [Hannah]" (1 Samuel 1:19 NIV). It was time.

God opened her womb; she "conceived and gave birth to a son. She named him Samuel, saying, 'Because I asked the LORD for him'" (v. 20). Had God forgotten her in the long delay? No. It was his preparation for her soul, to bring her to the place where the son she desired would be given back to God. Although Hannah did not know it yet, her son would have a significant calling in Israel. He would bring Israel back to God and prepare them to receive the king God was going to give them.

When it came time for the yearly sacrifice Elkanah went up with his family, but Hannah stayed home with Samuel. She said to her husband, "After the boy is weaned, I will take him and present him before the LORD, and he will live there always" (v. 22). The age of weaning was usually three years. This was a special time for Hannah to enjoy her son. She watched his first smile, saw him take his first steps, and heard his first words. But she had made a vow, and she was going to keep it. "After he was weaned, she took the boy with her, young as he was, along with a three-year-old bull . . . flour and a skin of wine, and brought him to the house of the LORD at Shiloh" (v. 24). After the sacrifice of the bull and the presentation of the other gifts, they brought the boy to Eli the priest. Hannah said to him, "As surely as you live, my lord, I am the woman who stood here beside you praying to the LORD. I prayed for this child, and the LORD has granted me what I asked of him. So now I give him to the LORD. For his whole life he will be given over to the LORD' " (vv. 26–28). And Samuel worshiped.

God had a special purpose in dealing with Hannah. She becomes a woman of faith and prayer. Her son, Samuel, becomes a man of prayer to bring the people of Israel back to God. Today we are not expected to leave a young child at the door of the church, but we are expected, in our hearts, to give our children to God. I think of Moses' mother putting her son in a basket and pushing the baby into the Nile River, expecting God to care for him. And God did. You know the history of how God prepared Moses to deliver God's people from the land of Egypt, the land of slavery.

Often as mothers we think it is all up to us, and then we are plunged into guilt and fear because of our failure. I watched my daughter Barbara's rebellion with the deepest fear. The promise that she was God's brought very little comfort. But there came a time when Jack and I prayed against the Enemy and truly believed that she belonged to God. We gave her to God unreservedly. Then we were free from any kind of manipulation to bring her back. We were free to love and accept her just as she was. We were filled with confidence in God's covenant promise that he would pursue her until he brought her to himself. And he did. Living in God's presence requires a constant submission to the will of the Father. It is a walk of faith characterized by putting our burdens, our joys, and our treasures at the foot of the cross every day.

HANNAH'S SONG

Again Hannah prays, and this time she sings. Her first prayer was one of agony and desperation. Now she prays in triumph and exaltation. This prayer is not about her. Now Hannah sees life as God sees it. He was with her in all the suffering that went on year after year. He had never forsaken her.

Her prayer is enforced by a vow. Not cutting Samuel's hair meant that he was dedicated to the Lord for the rest of his life. Her greatest sacrifice was to leave her son at the temple. If she had had children earlier without the long delay, there would have been no need to bring this young boy to serve God in the temple at such an early age. But, taught by the Spirit, Hannah now sings a song in which she speaks of her joy in the Lord. Through the years, God's people have found comfort from her song.

> My heart rejoices in the LORD; in the LORD my horn is lifted high.
> My mouth boasts over my enemies, for I delight in your
>   deliverance.
>
> There is no one holy like the LORD; there is no one besides you;
>   there is no Rock like our God.
>
> Do not keep talking so proudly or let your mouth speak such
>   arrogance,
> for the LORD is a God who knows, and by him deeds are
>   weighed.
>
> The bows of the warriors are broken, but those who stumbled
>   are armed with strength.
> Those who were full hire themselves out for food, but those who
>   were hungry hunger no more.
> She who was barren has borne seven children, but she who has
>   had many sons pines away.
>
> The LORD brings death and makes alive; he brings down to the
>   grave and raises up.
> The LORD sends poverty and wealth; he humbles and he exalts.
> He raises the poor from the dust and lifts the needy from the
>   ash heap; he seats them with princes and has them inherit a
>   throne of honor.
>
> For the foundations of the earth are the LORD's; upon them he
>   has set the world.
> He will guard the feet of his saints, but the wicked will be
>   silenced in darkness.

It is not by strength that one prevails; those who oppose the
  LORD will be shattered.
He will thunder against them from heaven; the LORD will judge
  the ends of the earth.

He will give strength to his king and exalt the horn of his
  anointed. (1 Samuel 2:1–10 NIV)

Hannah's praise did not dwell on the gift God had given her. Her praise was for the Giver of the gift. This is the delight of living in God's presence. She first praises him for who he is. She looks at who God is before she considers what he has done.

"There is no one holy like the LORD; there is no one besides you" (v. 2). He is holy because he is the absolutely independent and self-sufficient God. There is no other God. He is separate from sinners, yet he stoops to the hungry and needy. From him all goodness and truth flow.

"There is no Rock like our God" (v. 2). God is always dependable and trustworthy. Water came out of the rock in the wilderness to satisfy the thirst of over 1.5 million people. The rock that followed them was Christ. He still is the only one who can satisfy the deepest need of the heart. Believe this and you are living in God's presence.

Hannah speaks against the enemies of God. The accusations of our enemies do not define us because the Lord weighs the motives of the heart and acts according to his justice. We can trust the outworking of his plan. This is living in God's presence.

He delights in helping those who stumble. In fact, he strengthens them. He feeds the hungry. He gives the barren woman children, and even those with children are not satisfied unless they find their rest in him.

He is totally sovereign over death. We are bombarded with advice on how to live longer. We are filled with guilt when we haven't done what we should. God is sovereign over life and death. Knowing this truth frees us from guilt. The hairs of our head are numbered and so are our days. Believe this and you are living in God's presence.

"The LORD sends poverty and wealth; he humbles and he exalts. He raises the poor from the dust and lifts the needy from the ash heap; he seats them with princes and has them inherit a throne of honor" (vv. 7–8). If you sense that you are poor and needy with a sorrowful spirit like Hannah, then remember that Jesus is the Rock, the one who lifts up, sustains and strengthens. Believing this is living in his presence.

"It is not by strength that one prevails" (v. 9). Our own strength is not sufficient to stand against the enemies who oppose us and the Lord. He promises that they will be shattered. "He will thunder against them from heaven" (v. 10). He is the judge of all the earth. He fights our battles for us. Trust his sovereignty. He is good.

"He will give strength to his king and exalt the horn of his anointed" (v. 10). He will exalt the king he has promised to give to his people. Hannah sings of the future king. Her son Samuel anointed David to be king of Israel. David, a man after God's own heart, brought unity and peace to God's people. David's son Solomon was the wisest king who ever lived. Now someone greater than Solomon is here: Christ, God's anointed King (Matthew 12:42).

Christ the King has come. He did what Samuel, David, and Solomon could not do. They could not make our hearts right with God or build an everlasting kingdom. They could only be examples for us. Christ died, the just for the unjust, to bring us into God's presence. All of life is under his control. If this is so, why are we not content with his plan and purposes?

God desires our heart, but our vision is distorted. We look and judge the things that are seen; we follow the goals our culture sets before us; we let the cares of this world choke the Word; we fix our eyes on the creature rather than the Creator. We need a glimpse of another country.

HANNAH'S FAITH

Hannah leaves Samuel at the temple, returning home with joy and contentment. She had given God the treasure of her heart. God had taken away her reproach and taught her about his sovereign ways among men and nations. "The LORD was gracious to Hannah; she conceived and gave birth to three sons and two daughters. Meanwhile, the boy Samuel grew up in the presence of the LORD" (1 Samuel 2:21 NIV). Each year when Hannah came to the temple, she would bring Samuel a coat much like the priest wore. I am sure that Hannah continued to pray for her son through the years. Samuel at an early age learned to listen to God when God spoke to him in the temple. "The LORD was with Samuel as he grew up, and he let none of his words fall to the ground" (3:19 NIV). This is what you want to pray for your children. All Israel recognized that Samuel was a prophet of the Lord. He became a man of prayer and was God's appointed leader to bring Israel back to God. He anointed the first king, Saul, and later David.

I am drawn to Hannah because she is such a wonderful picture of God's ways. She learned, as Betty Herron did, that God is the first cause in all the affairs of life. He closes and opens the womb. He brings death and makes alive. He sends poverty and wealth; he humbles and exalts. He raises the poor and lifts the needy.

Out of Hannah's desperation she cried out to the only one who could help her. She learned to live in God's presence. She never knew how much her sorrow and her vow to give Samuel to God would influence the world for years to come. Her song is repeated in Psalm 113:7. Mary, the mother of Jesus, was also nourished by these words. She sings them when the angel announces that she is to be the mother of the Messiah.

Through the ages women with sorrowful spirits have taken courage and given the tragic and impossible circumstances of their lives to God. Spurgeon writes about Hannah, "Through her sorrowful spirit Hannah learned to pray. . . . Her appeal was to the Lord. She poured not out the secret of her soul into mortal ears, but spread her grief before God in His own house and in His own appointed manner! She was in bitterness of soul and prayed to the Lord! Bitterness of soul should always be thus sweetened."[4]

There are many who are going through difficult times. Some of you, like Hannah, have sorrowful hearts. Everywhere I go I meet those who are sorrowing in their hearts in difficult circumstances. Hannah teaches us that we are not dealing with a distant God who knows nothing of what being human, frail, and mortal means. We have a Great High Priest who has passed into the heavens praying for us. Alister McGrath writes, "It matters—it matters enormously—to know that God was present at Calvary. The cross tells us that God has been through the dark side of life, its pain and suffering. And so when we experience the darker side of life, we can turn to him in prayer, and in confidence that he knows what we are going through."[5] Jesus doesn't ask us to do something he hasn't done before us. He submitted to the will of the Father for the joy set before him—that of bringing us with him into the Father's presence.

Hannah learned through persecution, loss of identity,

perplexities, and hardships to live in God's presence and become a woman of prayer. Betty wrote, "God has given me great boldness in believing that he loves me and has the best plan. This gives me a lot of daily joy and little fear to know there is a greater master of my life than myself." Living in God's presence means to give up our own agendas and become dependent on the Man of Sorrows who is acquainted with grief. This same Jesus, now resurrected, is our High Priest praying for us. His Father and ours has a good plan for our lives.

19

Mary Was Given
an Impossible Task

Life is full of interruptions. These interruptions tell us that life is not what we hoped for. God interrupts our ordinary expectations, as cherished as they are, so that he might give us more of himself. He closed Hannah's womb so that he could move into her life with a kingdom vision. For Hannah it was a long interruption. Now we meet Mary, who is going to have many interruptions in her life. Following Mary through the books of Luke, John, and Acts, we find that God interrupts her life again and again. Through it all we find a woman who is learning about living in God's presence, a woman who is learning that nothing is impossible with God.

GOD INTERRUPTS WEDDING PLANS

Mary is engaged to Joseph. Like many a bride, she is already planning her wedding. Then the angel Gabriel visits her—a different type of wedding planner than you or I would hire. He tells her that she is the one chosen by God to bring the long-awaited Messiah into the world. She is not only favored by Joseph but now highly favored by God himself.

Her first reaction is to be greatly troubled. Her only question is, "How will this be?" She is told that "the Holy Spirit will come upon [her], and the power of the Most High will overshadow [her]" (Luke 1:34–35 NIV). Knowing that this meant she would be pregnant before she married Joseph, she must have wondered how Joseph would take this news. What would her family say? She obviously didn't spend a lot of time on her fears because she says, "I am the LORD's servant. May it be to me as you have said" (Luke 1:38 NIV). Her submission to God's plan brought her into God's presence. Submitting to the interruptions in our lives is living in God's presence.

God graciously gives Mary a human confirmation of the angel's words. Gabriel tells Mary that her relative Elizabeth is pregnant in her old age. He lets her know that "nothing is impossible with God" (1:37 NIV). The angel who visited Sarah hundreds of years earlier had asked, "Is anything too hard for the LORD?" (Genesis 18:14)—words that came with the announcement that she would bear a child at ninety years of age. Mary hurries to be with Elizabeth. When she enters her home, she is greeted with these astonishing words: "Blessed are you among women, and blessed is the child you will bear! But why am I so favored, that the mother of my LORD should come to me? As soon as the sound of your greeting reached my ears, the baby in my womb leaped for joy. Blessed is she who has believed that what the Lord has said to her will be accomplished!" (Luke 1:42–45 NIV). Mary is blessed because of her faith. God interrupts, and she responds with faith. She is walking in God's presence as she believes and submits to what God is doing.

Hannah sang of the coming King, and now the King is coming. Mary's prayer and song overflow as she walks in the presence of God. For us, too, prayer and rejoicing flow naturally from a heart of faith that says, "Let it be to me according to your word" (Luke 1:38). Mary's heart remembers Hannah's song as she sings:

> My soul glorifies the LORD and my spirit rejoices in God my
> Savior,
> for he has been mindful of the humble state of his servant.
> From now on all generations will call me blessed, for the
> Mighty One has done great things for me—holy is his name.
> His mercy extends to those who fear him, from generation to
> generation.
> He has performed mighty deeds with his arm; he has scattered
> those who are proud in their inmost thoughts.
> He has brought down rulers from their thrones but has lifted
> up the humble.
> He has filled the hungry with good things but has sent the rich
> away empty.
> He has helped his servant Israel, remembering to be merciful
> to Abraham and his descendants forever, even as he said to our
> fathers. (Luke 1:46–55 NIV)

Mary undoubtedly knew Hannah's story and the song she sang when she believed that God was going to give her a son. They both sing about the ways of God. He is holy. He scatters the proud, lifts the humble, fills the hungry, and sends the rich away empty. The sovereign God is in control over rulers, their thrones, and all the events of life. He is faithful to his promises to Abraham, Isaac, and Jacob. History moves under his control. Living in his presence means believing these truths.

The truths of the song Mary sang must have come alive to her after the birth of Jesus. The shepherds visit her with the news that a great company of angels appeared to them singing, "Glory to God in the highest, and on earth peace to men on whom his favor rests" (Luke 2:14 NIV). They were told that they would find the baby wrapped in cloths and lying in a manger. As she listens to their words, told with great excitement, she ponders her role as a woman highly favored by God to bring his Son into the world.

Eight days later, Jesus was presented in the temple for circumcision. Simeon, an older man who had been waiting to see the Lord's Christ, greets them. He blessed the family and said to Mary, "This child is destined to cause the falling and rising of many in Israel, and to be a sign that will be spoken against, so that the thoughts of many hearts will be revealed. And a sword will pierce your own soul too" (Luke 2:34–36 NIV). Up to this point in Mary's life, everything she experienced and heard was full of awe and glory; now she hears strange words about the piercing of her soul. She will learn that suffering is a part of life.

GOD INTERRUPTS MARY'S CHILD-REARING PLANS

When Jesus was twelve years old, he began to disengage himself from her that she might learn that he is not just her son but also her Savior.

The family had gone to Jerusalem for the Feast of the Passover. When the celebration was over, Mary and Joseph left for home, but Jesus stayed behind in the temple. When his mother and father missed him in the crowd they were traveling with, they returned to Jerusalem. "They found him in the temple courts, sitting among the teachers, listening to them and asking them questions. Everyone who heard him was amazed at his under-standing and his answers" (Luke 2:46–47 NIV), but not his parents. It seems as if Mary has lost her awe of who Jesus is because she does not stop to listen to his words. Did Mary forget Simeon's words that the one appointed for the rise and fall of many in Israel was indeed God's Son? Did she think God could be lost? It seems as if the wonder of who he was had become dim to Mary when she said, "Son, why have you treated us like this? Your father and I have been anxiously searching for you" (v. 48). Jesus makes no apologies but answers with a question: "Why were you searching for me? Didn't you know I had to be in my Father's house?" (v. 49).

At twelve years old, Jesus was already conscious of the unique relationship between himself and his Father in heaven. His entire life was controlled by his heavenly Father's will. Jesus reminded Mary and Joseph that he was responsible to only one Father—his Father in heaven. His allegiance was to him alone. He was also telling Mary that he had a mission. Mary seems to have forgotten this, losing the wonder she sang about when she visited Elizabeth. In losing focus, she has become anxious and fearful. She asks the wrong question, blaming him for her anxiety. Even as she is rebuked for forgetting who Jesus is and what he came to do, his grace toward her is evident. He returns home and is obedient to them, growing "in wisdom and stature, and in favor with God and men" (2:52). Mary again quietly treasures all these events in her heart. This was one of many painful interruptions that would come to Mary's life.

About eighteen years after this event, Jesus is declared by John the Baptist to be the Lamb of God that takes away the sin of the world. After Jesus is baptized by John, he attends a wedding with his mother and five of his disciples (John 2:1–10). His mother notices that they have run out of wine and tells Jesus. To run out of wine at a wedding in a Middle Eastern culture is a social embarrassment that brings shame to the host. I was not brought up in that culture, but I did run out of food at one daughter's wedding, and I felt deeply ashamed and embarrassed. It took me years to get over the guilt of that failure.

Jesus responds to Mary by saying something that sounds strange to our ears. "Dear woman, why do you involve me? My time has not yet come" (v. 4 NIV). He will say this many times before he finally says, "[My] time has come" (John 17:1 NIV). Richard John Neuhaus in his book *Death on a Friday Afternoon* writes, "Jesus has now no other life than what he calls 'my hour,' referring to his appointed mission. In relation to Jesus, there is no way to be part, to have part, except to take part in his 'hour.' There is no independent connection with Jesus, no connection apart from that mission, not even the connection of a mother with her son. Mary would come to understand this more fully at the foot of the cross, but she was learning it along the way to that climactic 'hour.' "[1]

Mary must have thought it was about time that Jesus let people know who he was and what he could do. Jesus, on the other hand, was so in tune with his heavenly Father that he wasn't going to do anything without hearing from him. Jesus would not be manipulated. Mary needed to know that she was not in charge of Jesus. In his love for her, he had to distance himself so that she would understand that, from now on, Jesus' relationship to her had to change. Even as Jesus challenges her, he does not disappoint. He quietly turns the water into wine, saving the host from embarrassment; indeed, the host is praised for saving the best wine for last.

Jesus' love never disappoints. We may not get what we want or think we need, but if he withholds it, it is always to change our misconceptions about himself, life, and our relationship to him.

Finding our rest as we live in the presence of God comes as we give up our misconceptions about God and what he should do for us. Notice that Mary says, "Do whatever he tells you" (John 2:5 NIV). When she says that, she is letting go of being in charge of the Savior of the world. His response to her letting go is to turn the water into wine. And the best wine is simply to be with him and to love what he loves. He always gives us more of himself as he draws us into his presence. Lilias Trotter, a missionary to Muslims in Algeria wrote, "Life is grandly simple when we reach that point, when the spirit of calculating results and consequences has been left behind and when God himself, and no mere experience, is our exceeding great reward."[2]

JESUS INTERRUPTS MARY'S FUTURE

Mary next appears in Luke 8, when she and her other sons come to visit Jesus. They find him teaching in a house so full of people that they can't get near him. Jesus is told, "Your mother and your brothers are standing outside, desiring to see you" (Luke 8:20). Jesus does not come out to see them, nor does he make the crowds move aside for his mother. He says to those listening, "My mother and brothers are those who hear the word of God and do it" (v. 21). This would seem rude if you didn't know who Jesus is and what he came to do. He came to establish a new family: a family he was going to give his life for, who would listen to and obey God's Word. Jesus was not dismissing his family's importance since he continued to care for Mary right up to the time of his death. However, with these words he made it clear that he was establishing a new family, and Mary and his earthly brothers would become a part of it. Created by the heavenly Father, the people who hear and do his words are now his new family. The natural family can never be more important than the family Jesus died for.

I meet people all over the world who are far more anxious about their immediate family than they are about the family God is building. I know fear and fear is what I hear. First John 4:18 says, "The one who fears is not made perfect in love" (NIV). You cannot live in God's presence when you are anxious and fearful about your family. The fear expresses itself in having such a tight control over the lives of your children that you don't leave room for the Spirit to work. I marvel at Hannah, who left her little boy in the care of a corrupt priest. I am sure she covered that little one in prayer. Hannah lived in God's presence, believing that God would take care of Samuel. Now Mary also had to let go of her hopes and dreams for her family. This could not have been easy for her.

Before fear invaded my life, I worked hard at building my family. I remember sitting in the back row of a church decades ago. I had two toddlers, a six-month-old baby, and I was pregnant with my daughter Barbara. Children's books and Cheerios kept the little ones quiet during the sermon. In the early years of child rearing, I didn't get too much out of the sermons, but that morning I heard God speak. A seminary professor was preaching on Psalm 127: "Children are a heritage from the LORD, the fruit of the womb a reward. Like arrows in the hand of a warrior are the children of one's youth. Blessed is the man who fills his quiver with them!" (Psalm 127:3–5). Those words sank into my heart and sustained me through the years when Jack was getting his education. I was truly blessed by God. My quiver was getting fuller. The professor said that this is the way God builds his kingdom. So we trained, nurtured, taught, loved, and played with our family. We expected God to provide all our needs and he did.

However, without realizing it, through the years I forgot the first part of the psalm: "Unless the LORD builds the house, those who build it labor in vain" (v. 1). Outwardly our training was successful. Our children did well in school; they could handle themselves in conversations with adults; they were well-mannered, obedient in the home, and they intellectually understood the gospel. I was building a family, and that family made me look good. I really thought that if I concentrated on right outward behavior, my children's hearts would change. I am not against the training of children; it is important and necessary to train them in God's ways. But it is the greatest pride to think that our efforts will change a child's heart. It is all of grace! My wrong perception of parenting was shattered when Barbara, our fourth child, stormed out of our lives, wanting nothing more to do with us, the church, and especially God. I was devastated, hurt, confused, and full of fear.

Mary must have felt hurt at Jesus' seeming rejection when he did not make time to see her. With Barbara's rebellion, I too felt abandoned by God, but I had to learn that God was going to interrupt my kingdom building in order to build his kingdom. How was I going to stand in God's presence when it seemed as if he weren't present? Both Hannah and Mary sing about God humbling the proud and lifting up the needy. God started by humbling my pride and showing me my need. I had no resources to change Barbara, and the ministry Jack and I had to people living in our home also became too much for me to handle. Life was out of control. I couldn't seem to fix anything, especially myself. Finally I came to the place where I wasn't even sure God existed. Bringing me to that place of total need was God's preparation for me to hear the Spirit speak peace to my heart.

I was at a Communion service when my heart broke over my

sins of pride, self-righteousness, and presumption. The Father opened my eyes to grace. The blood of Christ cleansed the intense, self-centered moralism that dominated my life. Before this happened, my thinking centered on moral failure and success rather than sin and grace. I had thought of sin as a social failure on my part or on others'. I felt condemned by these failures, but I defended my shabby record by blaming others when things didn't go the way I wanted. Then, having tried to clear my conscience by blaming others, I made myself busy with work and duty. I always wanted God to buoy up my strength and enhance my good record. With a new clarity I saw in the Communion service that Christ had kept the requirements of God's law for me, and the only worthwhile record was his. His obedient life and death for my sins were my only hope.

Until then I had never seen or admitted that I had neither strength nor righteousness. I now brought real sins to a real Savior and I was forgiven. It is awesome to be loved so unconditionally by a holy, righteous God. This is what I missed in my parenting. I was not a humble, needy sinner before my children. Since I did not see myself as a sinner, I did not know how to bring them to Christ. When I started to change, Barbara began to have hope that Christianity might be true. There came a time when I gave all control of my children to God. They were his, and he was to do with them as he willed. My job was to pray for them. And God in his own time brought each of them to himself. I tell others that their efforts at parenting are like putting the water into the water pot to let Jesus turn the water into wine. This is what he did for my family.

I still thought that my primary work was to be with my immediate family. I had to travel to Uganda many times before I could see what Jesus was telling Mary: Jesus' mother and brothers are those who hear God's Word and do it. I am deeply thankful for what God has done in the lives of my children and grandchildren, but my life and theirs are wrapped up in God's worldwide family of those who hear the Word of God and do it. Jesus again refers to the family he came to build in Luke 11. As Jesus was talking about evil spirits, a woman in the crowd called out, "Blessed is the mother who gave you birth and nursed you" (Luke 11:27 NIV). Jesus did not deny it, but he broadened the scope of the blessing. He widened the sphere of true blessedness to include all genuine believers. Mary's blessedness did not consist exclusively in the fact that she had given birth to Jesus but that she had listened carefully to the Word of God and surrendered herself to his will. Mary is truly a blessed woman as she takes her place with us when Jesus again says, "Blessed rather are those who hear the word of God and obey it" (v. 28). Ask God to give you grace to accept the interruptions of your life and to give you a heart to listen and surrender to his Word. This is living in God's presence.

GOD INTERRUPTS MARY'S FUTURE

The next time we see Mary, her soul is pierced by seeing her son crucified on the cross. When Jesus was presented as a newborn in the temple, Mary had been told by Simeon that a sword would pierce her soul. How little had the young mother realized that Simeon was looking ahead to the crucifixion of her son! As Jesus is hanging in shame on the cross, she hears his words to those who are crucifying him, "Father, forgive them, for they know not what they do" (Luke 23:34). She must have known that soon she too would have to forgive those who were putting to death her innocent son—the son she had bathed, nursed, and raised.

As she stands next to John at the cross, Mary hears Jesus say, "'Dear woman, here is your son,' and to the disciple, 'Here is your mother'" (John 19:26–27 NIV). Her heart must have broken at his suffering, yet at the same time she was comforted that he had not forgotten her. At the time of his deepest agony, he was caring for her. What manner of love is this? With these words, he is moving her out of her immediate family to his larger family. Jesus knew how much she was suffering and how lonely she would be when he was gone. He had neither silver nor gold to leave her, but he would provide a home and tender care for her as long as she required them. And "from that time on, this disciple took her into his home" (v. 27 NIV).

If John took her home at that moment, she did not hear Jesus' cry of anguish when the words, "My God, my God, why have you forsaken me?" were wrung from his lips (Mark 15:34). This is the only time in Jesus' life that he calls his heavenly Father "God." From this time until Jesus cries, "It is finished!" he is bearing the awful wrath of God because of our sins. The greatest interruption in all of history is the breaking of the fellowship between the heavenly Father and his Son, Jesus. Joni Eareckson Tada in *When God Weeps* imagines the Father's wrath being poured out on his beloved Son:

> They lift the cross. God is on display . . . and can scarcely breathe. But these pains are a mere warm-up to his other and growing dread. . . . He *feels* dirty. Human wickedness starts to crawl upon his spotless being—the living excrement from our souls. The apple of his Father's eye turns brown with rot. His Father! He must face his Father like this!
>
> From heaven the Father now rouses himself like a lion disturbed, shakes his mane, and roars against the shriveling

remnant of a man hanging on a cross. *Never* has the Son seen the Father look at him so, never felt even the least of his hot breath. But the roar shakes the unseen worlds and darkens the visible sky. The Son does not recognize these eyes.

"Son of Man! Why have you behaved so? You have cheated, lusted, stolen, gossiped—murdered, envied, hated, lied. You have cursed, robbed, overspent, overeaten—fornicated, disobeyed, embezzled, and blasphemed.... I hate, I loathe these things in you! ... Can you not feel my wrath?" The Father watches as his heart's treasure, the mirror-image of himself, sinks drowning into raw, liquid sin. Jehovah's stored rage against humankind from every century explodes in a single direction.

"[My God, my God,] why have you forsaken me?" But heaven stops its ears. The Son stares up at the One who cannot, who will not, reach down or reply. Two eternal hearts tear—their intimate friendship shaken to the depths. The Trinity had planned it.... The Father accepted [the Son's] sacrifice for sin and was satisfied. The Rescue was accomplished.[3]

"It is finished" was his cry. Finished was the work the Father had given him to do. Finished was the beauty of a perfect life. Finished was the work of our redemption. He had done all that was required to reconcile the world to God and to make an end of sin. There is nothing left for us to do but to trust the results of Christ's finished work. Through the Eternal Spirit, Jesus offered himself without sin to God. By that one sacrifice he took the wrath we deserved. There can now be no condemnation for you. God can never again be angry with you if you are in Christ. This is often hard for people to hear. Alister McGrath writes,

The cross of Christ stands as a solemn and powerful reminder that God himself was prepared to suffer in order to redeem his world, and that he expects his people to share the same commitment and pain as they share in the task of restoring a fallen world. . . . We are not dealing with a distant God who knows nothing of what being human, frail and mortal means. He knows and understands. So we can "approach the throne of grace with confidence" (Hebrews 4:16). . . . [W]e can turn to him in prayer, and in confidence that he knows what we are going through. It makes prayer at times of sadness and suffering so much more meaningful and real—as it is meant to be.[4]

Now we have a High Priest who can sympathize with our weakness. He was tempted in all ways that we are, yet he did not sin. The invitation to all whose lives are being interrupted by suffering is to "approach the throne of grace with confidence, so that we may receive mercy and find grace to help us in our time of need" (Hebrews 4:16 NIV).

Mary is truly blessed. She is blessed because she brought the Son of God into the world. She is an example of one who listened and obeyed as she heard him speak. She also teaches us about suffering. It is hard to live in God's presence if you are fearful and anxious as she was when she found Jesus in the temple. It is hard to live in God's presence if you don't submit to the hard circumstances of your life. Richard John Neuhaus writes, "Mary learned the hard love of letting go, the love that is forged in surrender to a love greater than her own, the love that grows beyond all possessing."[5]

Suffering makes us better listeners when God speaks. It makes us long to be in his presence. Jesus' sacrifice is what makes it possible for us to be in God's presence. Suffering is more precious and much sweeter when we remember this.

I have dates listed next to certain passages in my Bible. They have to do with how these verses helped me through the struggles of life, ministry, and loneliness after Jack's death. Next to Jeremiah 18:1–6 are three dates. One is 1996, the year Jack died; one is 1998, two years later when I was speaking in Nashville; and the third is January 2000 in London. Why this passage and why these dates? This is the passage: "'Arise [Rose Marie], and go down to the potter's house, and there I will let you hear my words.' So I went down to the potter's house, and there he was working at his wheel. And the vessel he was making of clay was spoiled in the potter's hand, and he reworked it into another vessel, as it seemed good to the potter to do. . . . [God said] 'Behold, like the clay in the potter's hand, so are you in my hand.'"

On each date listed next to these verses, I had to come to a deeper submission to the will of God in taking Jack to be with him. In my continuing submission to his will, God was remaking me in the way that pleased him even if I didn't understand the reasons or even see any changes. But as I again accepted his will, sweet peace came. I will probably have to submit yet again—there is room for more dates!

Why suffering? Why the interruptions of God? Suffering gets rid of the dross of all the worldly supports we foolishly invent for our faith. Without realizing it, we often allow these supports to take God's place. Suffering strips away our assurance that life is under our control and that we are the ones who can fix others and ourselves. Suffering brings us face to face with God. With all the other props stripped away, we learn to trust God and lean on him alone. This is how we live in his presence.

MARY PRAYING

Our response to living in God's presence is prayer. We are invited to come to the throne of grace with the trials we cannot handle; the temptations that overcome us; painful, unresolved, and often broken relationships; unexplained hardships; deep, hurtful disappointments; and out-of-control circumstances. Coming to the throne, we find grace to help in time of need. We find grace because our Great High Priest has experienced every temptation and trial we face. Jesus bore the Father's wrath, so it is not a throne of condemnation or judgment—it is a throne of grace.

How do we live in the presence of God in the hardships of life? Let's look at our final picture of Mary in Acts 1. We find her and her sons with the disciples in the upper room, devoting themselves to prayer (v. 14). Before Jesus ascended into heaven, he told them to wait for the promised the Holy Spirit. He had promised his disciples that he would ask the Father for another Helper to be with them forever, the Spirit of truth (John 14:16–18). He told them, "He dwells with you and will be in you. I will not leave you as orphans; I will come to you. . . . The Helper, the Holy Spirit, whom the Father will send in my name, he will teach you all things and bring to your remembrance all that I have said to you" (John 14:17–18, 26).

We are adopted into the family of God. We are now as highly favored as Mary was. We are no longer slaves but heirs of God, with all the rights and privileges of children of the Living God. Our first meeting with Mary included a prayer, and our final picture has her praying too. This is how the Spirit leads us into his presence.

THE ONGOING STORY

Jesus said, "The kingdom of heaven is like a grain of mustard seed that a man took and sowed in his field. It is the smallest of all seeds, but when it has grown it is larger than all the garden plants and becomes a tree, so that the birds of the air come and make nests in its branches" (Matthew 13:31–32).

The mustard seed for the planting and growth of WHM began in 1975 when a Ugandan pastor fled the persecution of Idi Amin, came to study at Westminster Theological Seminary, and began worshiping at New Life Church. Four years later, when Amin was driven from power, our friend Kefa Sempangi returned home to help Uganda rebuild. He wanted to preach the Word and gather God's people for worship after hiding for years from Amin's brutality.

Kefa kept calling my husband saying, "You must come to Uganda and help establish a church like New Life Church. You must bring young men to help with the orphans who have lost families these last ten years." Kefa kept saying, "You must come, but it still is not safe." Finally in November of 1979 he said, "It is safe. COME."

Jack told me later, "I cried for two weeks because I really didn't want to go." He was mostly afraid of getting sick. I didn't want to go either. I thought I might die there. Well, we did go, and we both got sick, but we didn't die! Overall, we were certainly a picture of "not by might, nor by power, but by my Spirit, says the LORD of hosts" (Zechariah 4:6)! Four young men joined us, including our son-in-law Bob Heppe.

Preaching went on daily in the marketplace, orphans became Christians, a church was planted, and leaders were trained. After three months we returned home, but Jack couldn't wait to return. To my surprise, I felt the same way. The mustard seed was sprouting.

Our trips continued and several young men stayed for longer periods, working with orphans, establishing businesses, and working with churches. Soon other U.S. churches were interested in going to Uganda. It became evident that the work was becoming too big for New Life Church to administer alone. In a story too long to tell here, WHM was born in 1983.

Even then, work had already begun in Ireland. As far back as 1949, Jack had wanted to go to Ireland as a missionary. This didn't work out for him, but he never forgot the country. In 1977, Jack and I took a team of twenty-three young men and women from New Life Church to work alongside a Baptist church in the middle of Dublin. The church continued to invite us, and every year a team from New Life went to do evangelism. In 1983, two New Life families moved there permanently, and Ireland became WHM's second field.

The mustard seed continued to grow. Our next field was Amsterdam where the church plant is now led by Dutch Christians. London soon followed. From London, we are also reaching into India. All told, since 1994, nine mission fields have been added to WHM. Each one is unique.

And what has happened in Uganda where everything started? God brought many WHM missionaries to Uganda's western mountains. Churches have been planted and a school opened. A medical team meets many needs, the New Testament has been translated into Lubwisi, and clean water has come into the community.

Today, the mustard seed has grown into a tree through which nineteen nations of the world are hearing the gospel. We have much to be thankful for. I celebrate what God has done through our weakness, driving us to prayer to seek his glory.

This section includes talks and reflections from recent years that I hope reflect the weakness and the glory, the dependence on prayer, and the joy of promises fulfilled. God has truly done "exceedingly abundantly" above all that we could ask or think (Ephesians 3:20).

NEVER UNDERESTIMATE THE POWER OF THE SEED.

The Ongoing Story

20

The Power of Weakness

I was in London when I attended a three-day conference on "A Christian Response to Islam in Britain." The theme was "Faith, Power, and Weakness." There were about fifteen converted Muslims in attendance. The devotions they gave were very good. One of the men said, "The same person who gave us the Great Commandment also gave us the Great Commission." He said this to the "bridge builders," who make strong friendships with Muslims but often stop there. That statement was worth the whole conference.

Yet the conference was hard for me. I wasn't feeling well, and I missed Jack. I was surrounded by people who seemed to know what they were doing, and I wondered what I was doing there. At one point I wanted to get up and shout, "Is no one here weak?" It didn't seem that way. During the closing session, one of the conference coordinators said that she was burned out in her ministry with Muslims. I went to her later and thanked her for all her work and also for her closing remarks. I said, "I would have liked to have heard more about weakness."

My friend Andi Brindley sent me a concise summary of things God has taught her: "Welcome trials as friends; the way up is down; enemies are to be loved; hardship is ultimately about something good; worldly wisdom is really foolishness; our hope is not in the relief of our temporal suffering but in knowing the voice of God in the midst of affliction; your greatest strength is found in weakness." These were timely words to me as I attended the conference.

WEAKNESS

At the conference I had taken copious notes and collected a lot of data. Upon arriving home I discovered that I had misplaced my diary, which contained all my notes. I called the conference phone number but no one had found it. However, a few days later I received a call from someone who returned it to me in London.

The evening my notebook was returned, I went on the London Underground to meet someone for dinner. I had an hour to read through the last two years of journaling. The recurring theme was weakness, faith, and power.

The entry for October 18, 1997, reads: "I am going to speak today at a morning tea in a PCA church in Newark, Delaware. I dreamt last night about a dark shroud in the room. It was so real it woke me up. Then I went back to sleep to dream about funerals." A battle was going on. That morning I tried to find in 2 Corinthians where Paul writes: "The weapons we fight with are not weapons of the world . . . [the weapons we fight with] have divine power to demolish strongholds" (2 Corinthians 10:4–5 NIV). As I fruitlessly looked for the passage in chapter 11, I came upon something I needed to read—Paul's confession of weakness: "Who is weak, and I do not feel weak? . . . If I must boast, I will boast of the things that show my weakness" (11:29–30 NIV). Continuing into the chapter I read, "I will not boast about myself, except about my weaknesses" (12:5 NIV).

I knew I was in a battle, so it was helpful to read about Paul's weakness and to know that this is where I was. I went to the tea in weakness, taking along a praying friend. We prayed against Satan's devices and against the effect of the dream of the night before. We asked God for cleansing, for love for the women to whom I was speaking, and for joy as we served Christ. A few days later the woman who invited me called and said, "Your speaking made such an impact on the lives of the women." Weakness was turned to strength. I was learning: (1) I am weak; (2) It is necessary that I be weak; (3) It is important that my weakness shows; (4) When I am weak, then I am strong; (5) I need the prayers of God's people.

Spurgeon said in his sermon, "Paradox": "We are strong when, under a sense of absolute inability, we depend wholly upon God. . . . Only the seed which the Creator puts into the hand of our weakness will produce a harvest. . . . When a man is weak, then is he strong, because *he is sure to pray* and prayer is power. . . . The dead weight of [our] weakness makes [us] hold [Christ] as an anchor holds a ship. . . . When we are weak we are strong, again, because then *we are driven away from self to God.*"[1]

The weakness Paul talks about is a weakness that despairs of self and depends totally on Christ. The "dead weight of my weakness" made me hold onto Christ and his Word and rely on the prayers of others.

The wrong kind of weakness—presumptive weakness or despairing weakness—centers on self. *Presumptive weakness* is when I am strong in myself. I think, "I have the ability, the gifts, the understanding, the wisdom to get the job done or get on with life." But it is impossible to fully trust in God while you still cling to something in yourself. Then there is *despairing weakness*, where I look at my feeble resources and discover that they are insufficient and therefore believe that there is no hope.

In both cases we have forgotten the gospel. The gospel is all about a poor beggar finding bread. We forget that Christ died for sinners. We don't see our need for forgiveness and grace because in both cases we are concentrated on SELF. But we cannot share the gospel out of strength. True weakness is born out of a deep sense of inadequacy and need, which drives us to Christ and unleashes all the redeeming energy of God's grace in our lives.

Grace is all the apostle Paul needed to deal with his thorn in the flesh; and grace is all I needed to live without my husband.

FAITH

At the time of Jack's death I was reading Jeremiah's instructions to the people Nebuchadnezzar had carried into exile. He wrote: "This is what the LORD Almighty, the God of Israel, says to all those I carried into exile from Jerusalem to Babylon: 'Build houses and settle down; plant gardens and eat what they produce. . . . Also, seek the peace and prosperity of the city to which I have carried you into exile. Pray to the LORD for it, because if it prospers, you too will prosper' " (Jeremiah 29:4–5, 7 NIV).

As a widow, I identified with God's people who had lost so much. However, I knew I had not lost my identity as a daughter of my heavenly Father. God's message for me was clear: "Keep doing by faith what you were doing before Jack died. Only now *I* am your husband." As I moved out into teaching, mentoring, and speaking, God turned my weakness into strength. Because I knew I was weak, I constantly asked people to pray that God would fill the water jar—me—and turn the water into wine. And he did.

As I ministered, I leaned heavily on Christ, his Word, and the prayers of family and friends. But life isn't all ministry, is it? I felt needy all the time. A friend wrote, "Grief is an incredible journey. Seemingly it takes side trips and detours and carries us over many of the same roads over and over, all the while demanding so much energy—emotional and physical. Continue to saturate yourself in the Word. The Lord will provide a shield around you. He will continue to be your strength according to his Word." This I continued to do.

The side trips and detours of grief and suffering often reveal hidden sin patterns. Here are some of mine.

Self-centeredness. Grief and suffering leave us with the sense that life is out of control. This is how an orphan thinks: Life consciously or unconsciously is centered on personal autonomy and moral willpower, with grace understood as God maintaining your own strength—not as his transforming power. Turning in on myself was a major sin pattern. When I realized this, I knew I had no power to deal with it. I asked others to pray for deliverance and a clearer focus on Jesus, whose blood cleanses from all sin.

Unbelief. Is God's plan a good plan? Would God be with me as he had been with Jack? Days often began with a heavy heart. Would God be with me in the incredible times of loneliness? In the same passage where Jeremiah writes to the exiles about what they are to do, he reassures them with these words: "'For I know the plans I have for you,' declares the LORD, 'plans to prosper you and not to harm you, plans to give you hope and a future'" (Jeremiah 29:11 NIV). I had never connected this verse with the exiles, but then I had never experienced this kind of exile. The struggle with unbelief ebbs and flows. Again I asked others to pray for deliverance and a clearer focus on Jesus, whose blood cleanses from all sin. I believed the promise.

In Hebrews 11 I read that through faith kingdoms were conquered, weakness was turned to strength, the weak became powerful in battle, and foreign enemies were routed (Hebrews 11:33–34). This is a weakness and a faith worth boasting about!

POWER

As I read the Word and friends prayed, the Spirit powerfully moved in my heart. One Sunday, the sermon was from Isaiah, "You will go out in joy and be led forth in peace; the mountains and hills will burst into song before you, and all the trees of the field will clap their hands" (Isaiah 55:12 NIV). The Spirit applied God's Word to my heart. I left church that morning and by faith I made plans to "go out" to London. That week two ministry friends called. As I shared the call of God with them, they agreed God was leading me. This was God's human confirmation that I was following the leading of the Spirit. When I am weak, then I am strong.

At first, because of speaking engagements, I could only go to London for a few months at a time. However, the Spirit knew I needed deeper heart instruction about life without Jack and what his kingdom plans were. This came when I was speaking at a women's retreat in Florida. I was reading in John 12 the words: "The hour has come" (v. 23). Up to this point Jesus had repeatedly said, "My hour has not yet come" (John 2:4; 7:6, 30; 8:20). Now the Greeks wanted to see Jesus, and this was the signal from the Father that the hour had come for the kernel of wheat to fall into the ground and die. What impacted my heart was the fact that the nations had come to see Jesus. Now I was going to London where God had brought the nations. Through faith, weakness was turned to strength. I knew God would sovereignly bring the nations to me and the team in London. This is what he did. Soon I was involved in the lives of Saroj, a Hindu lady; Rita, her daughter; Shinder, a former Sikh now in a Radha Soami group; and Piya, whose father is a Buddhist and whose mother was a professing Christian.

Weakness, faith, power: that is how the kingdom of God moves into enemy territory. Missionary colleagues Paul and Lynn Leary wrote in their prayer letter: "It is hard to give you the full picture of what God is doing here. Instead we are grateful for the strength of God's grip on our lives. We are more aware of how he is holding onto us than we are of our ability to hold onto him. Our weekly times for team prayer have been a continual source of strength and joy as we make it through our week."

In response to my report of spending a day at Hampton Court with Shinder, my friend Andi wrote:

I think the enemy keeps us hanging back from ministry and relationships by leading us to believe that all that can be accomplished is what we feel capable of accomplishing, based on our perception of our strength and ability. So we wait to *feel* strong or enthusiastic, thinking this is evidence of God's strength. *Then* we step out. But I think believing grace is enough. . . . I think about your trip to Hampton Court with Shinder. You felt weak when it came to being with her, caring for her, sharing the gospel with her. You went ahead anyway, acknowledging your weakness, and God was strong. . . . There were the tapestries depicting the scenes of Jesus' ministry to women . . . the guard who prompted more sharing . . . you were able to describe the scenes on these tapestries to her . . . the gospel was preached anyway, even though you went in weakness. God's strength came through beyond just making you feel strong. In fact you went home and doubted your ability to describe these scenes well enough!!

Spurgeon writes:

Very well, then, let us pick up our tools and go to our work rejoicing, feeling—Well, I may be weaker, or I may be stronger in myself, but my strength is in my God. If I should ever become stronger, then I must pray for a deeper sense of weakness, lest I become weak through my strength. And if I should ever become weaker than I am, then I must hope and believe that I am really becoming stronger in the Lord. Whether I am weak or strong, what matters it? He who never fails and never changes will perfect his strength in my weakness, and this is glory to me.[2]

21

Contentment: Living in God's Presence

LIVING WITHIN GOD'S BOUNDARIES

Jack and I started married life in San Francisco, California, with some very concrete goals. Jack was to finish university—he had three years to go. I was not to work outside the home—I was finishing my education. We would let God choose the timing of our children as it pleased him. We lived on one hundred dollars a month. This covered a twenty-dollar room in a boarding house, food, and transportation across San Francisco Bay to my last semester at the University of California. We were not to go into debt or borrow money. *I was content.*

Three months later, I was pregnant with our first daughter. When the semester ended in May, Jack and I planned to go to Oregon to work on a fire lookout. But we had no money for bus fare. As we were considering our trip north, someone knocked on the door and asked if we could take a car to Jack's hometown. He would pay for gas. Jack grew up on the Oregon coast in a small fishing village called Gold Beach. We gave up our room, stored our wedding gifts, and headed north. We camped in the redwoods for one night—my favorite place in California—and delivered the car three blocks from Jack's mother's home.

That summer we lived in one room on top of the mountain—glass all around. We had free "housing" and enough money to pay for the groceries that were delivered to our lookout. I learned to cook and bake on a wood stove and to travel down the mountain to get clean, fresh water from a mountain stream for washing and drinking. I also learned how to shoot a .22 rifle. Since we had a lot of empty cans, Jack taught me how to shoot to hit.

Mice were plentiful and came out at night to scamper around our room. Often Jack chased them with a broom or tried to shoot them. Finally I said, "Why don't we take the tops of the empty cans and nail them over every opening or crevice?" He said, "They could never get through those cracks." But we did nail everything shut and the mice stopped coming. *I was content.*

After the summer we traveled back to San Francisco. Jack still had two more years of school. But where were we going to live? We found a one-room apartment with a small kitchen for thirty dollars a month. Jack was now working as a manager in the school cafeteria, earning a little more money so we could afford the ten-dollar increase. I wanted my first baby to be born in the University of California Hospital, so I went to register. I was told that I couldn't afford the eighty-dollar bill; my husband wasn't making enough money. I replied, "If I pay twenty dollars a month until the baby is due, will you accept me?" They did and my daughter Roseann was born there. I did need this hospital. It was a difficult delivery, and I lost a lot of blood. After two weeks I developed a breast infection, and it took me many months to recover. *But I was content.*

The next summer we again traveled to Oregon to work on a lookout. This time we camped on the ground below because the lookout was too small to sleep in. The forest service set up a tent for us and again brought groceries. We traveled up the mountain each day, Jack carrying Roseann, now five months old, with our food and water for the day. Her bed was a banana box in the lookout. I was now pregnant with Ruth.

Returning again to San Francisco, we needed a place to live. This was in 1951 when rent control was still in effect. Some people in our small church were having trouble with their landlord over rent control and didn't want to live in their house until the matter was settled. It was a beautiful old seven-bedroom house near the Twin Peaks tunnel. I loved it. They offered it to us for twenty-two dollars a month. We still had no car, no insurance, no bank account, no savings, and no phone. *But I was content.*

Ruth was born in March 1952. Now I had two little ones to care for in this big, beautiful house. It was a happy time. Jack was still going to school. I had no washer so I boiled all the diapers. We had a small icebox and, when we could afford it, a block of ice was delivered. My food budget was ten dollars a week. That year we did not return to Oregon, but after two years we had to move because the rent control problems were settled. But where would we go? Two days before we had to move, someone in our church offered us a three-bedroom apartment for thirty dollars a week. Here Paul was born, and Jack finished university. *I was content.*

When Paul was three months old, we moved to Philadelphia so that Jack could attend Westminster Seminary. We lived in Germantown in a second-floor apartment with four rooms. This is

where our fourth child, Barbara, was born. Our sleeping arrangements were interesting. Roseann was in the front room, Paul was
in the kitchen, Ruth was in the second bedroom and Barb was in
the hallway. Moving to Philadelphia was a cross-cultural experience. In addition, winters were cold; summers were hot. I was
used to the gentle climate of San Francisco. But God provided
every need. *I was content.*

Living in Philadelphia was not easy. Jack took public transportation to seminary, often standing for long hours in the win-
try cold waiting for the bus. After two years, he became ill and I
was also very weary. We decided to return to California. Barbara
was almost a year old; Paul was two, Ruth three, and Roseann
four. Jack applied to teach English in a Christian school in central
California in a predominantly Dutch community. We now lived
on $285 a month, enough to pay for food and rent. We squeezed
into a two-bedroom home. Our house was not on the side of
town where the wealthy farmers lived but on the side where the
one-room jail was. We had no phone, no car, no bank account,
no insurance, and no credit cards. But because Jack taught at the
high school, our children were able to attend Christian school for
free. *I was content.*

WANTING MORE

After two years, I began to think that our house was too small
and that we should find a bigger house. I didn't really fit into the
Dutch community, and Roseann was in bed much of the time
with a heart problem. For the first time, I wanted more than I
had. *A restless discontent began to settle in my heart.*

A family gave us a car. We moved into an old farmhouse about ten miles out of town, with lots of room inside and out. But the downside was that we now had a car we couldn't afford to repair, and it needed gas that wasn't included in the budget.

Looking back, it is interesting for me to see the influence that my parents' view of money had on me. My father was very frugal. He never went into debt and never had a credit card. Although he never sat down and gave me a lesson on money, I learned very early that you live on what you make. This had a profound effect on me, so when I didn't quite make it money-wise, I felt I had failed, and guilt began to replace faith. There was nothing wrong with wanting a bigger house, but what I did not do was wait for God to provide it. A few months after we moved, a large home became available for teachers. I should have waited.

WHEN UNWANTED THINGS INTRUDE

My discontent went deeper when Jack made a decision to plant a church in Stockton, California. I did not want to be a pastor's wife. My plan was to be the wife of a professor. I didn't know how to deal with this new reality.

It was a difficult church plant, and there was not much support for Jack from other pastors in dealing with the problems he faced. With the church occupying his time and attention, plus a fifty-mile commute to the Christian school, Jack had little energy left to help me at home. I missed his support with the children. But above all I missed the sense of God's presence. *I was no longer content.*

Keren was born in April 1960. The summers in Stockton were hot—often over 107 degrees. We had no fan, and the refrigerator was too small to hold ice. Then the one dear friend I had in the Dutch community died. Another friend from out of state came to attend the funeral and visit me. It was one of those very hot days. I was sitting in the kitchen, nursing Keren with my sweat dripping down on her forehead. My friend said, "Rose Marie, you shouldn't have to live this way."

That did it. I believed the voice from the pit. Now anger was added to discontent. "She's right," I thought. "I should not have to live this way." Now I could blame someone—my husband. It was all Jack's fault! I continued to listen to Satan whisper, "Your only hope is to tough it out and do your duty. God will not come through for you. You are a victim of Jack's decision."

Even if we don't believe, God is still faithful. He was so to us. Our children were able to attend Christian school. They found friends in the neighborhood and in the church. There was a city pool close by where we could swim for free in the hot days of summer.

Every afternoon I walked to a nearby bakery and bought pastry so that I had tea and cake ready when the children came home. I started to read the classics to them. It was a sweet family time. We had no TV, so reading was a great way to connect with them. We had a fun family night every Friday when the children made up plays and acted them out.

Until this time I believed I was in partnership with God: He would provide, and I would believe. Life was simple. But when the direction of my life changed—now a pastor's wife—and income was insufficient, I lost the sense of partnership. I lost it in anger and rebellion, blaming Jack.

THE CONTENTMENT OF FAITH

Years later in a quiet moment, when I was reflecting on this time in my life, I sensed God saying quietly, "Rose Marie, I gave you a family. You believed that I would take care of every need, and I did. Then, when I called Jack into ministry, you rebelled at my calling and refused to believe I could be with you in the next stage of your life. This was a time for you to enter more deeply into my plan and you refused. My plan for you and your family is wise and good, and only grief can come when you do not accept and submit to it. Your lack of love for people and your rebellion against me were exposed. But you had such tight control over your life, and you were so sure about how it should work, you didn't take the time to listen to me."

No audible voice spoke to me. These were simply strong convictions controlling my mind. But they had the ring of God's truth in them.

Jack and I did become partners when we took troubled people into our home and when we started New Life Church, but there was still something missing in me. I had not yet reached the level of deep contentment. My understanding of the cross, of the sacrifice of Jesus, of the cup he drank of the Father's wrath against sin—against *my* sin—needed to shape the core of my life. It was there to some extent, but the foundation of trust needed to go deeper into what it cost Jesus.

God knew this and because of his steadfast love (certainly not any work or effort on my part) at a Communion table he revealed his justice, his righteousness, and his incomprehensible love. I saw clearly that if I had been at the crucifixion, playing the victim in my cold rebellion and anger, I would have plunged the spear into his side. But when the bread was broken and the wine tasted during the Lord's Supper that day, I brought my rebellion, pride, arrogance, selfishness, hypocrisy, pretense, and outward conformity to Jesus. He exchanged it for an untarnished righteousness, making me forever his child, his daughter. I was exposed and forgiven at the same time. I was free to forgive Jack and to ask for his forgiveness. This was a defining moment, and it continues to shape my life to this day.

Do I still need the gospel? All the time! My heart drifts as easily as an autumn leaf on a windy day. I have a supportive network of children, grandchildren, and friends who pray for me. Without their prayers I would go back to all my old coping strategies and lose the blessing of the presence of Christ. There is a big difference! I really can go with boldness to the throne of grace. The Holy Spirit is the resident Counselor and I truly depend on his power to convict of sin, teach me, and reveal Christ to my needy heart.

After my encounter with grace at the Communion table, my life became predictable in a different way. I was no longer living like an orphan, trying to find out who I was and where I belonged. Now I could freely partner with Jack in what was close to his heart—reaching the world for Christ. *Again, I was content.*

There had been many upheavals in my life: living with a schizophrenic mother; my father's death; rebellion of children; troubled people living in our home; living in Uganda; Jack's heart attack; his brushes with death when he had lymphoma and, a few years later, a stroke. But the biggest change came in 1996. We were in Spain when Jack underwent open-heart surgery. But his heart was too damaged; he never made it through the week and died on April 8. As the psalmist writes, "The earth gives way, though the mountains be moved into the heart of the sea" (Psalm 46:2). That is how I felt.

Old fears surfaced. I felt alone. But I found I had a purpose in my life that had developed under Jack's mentoring. Suffering can easily turn the heart inward, trying to guard against further pain. But I began to see the world with the eyes of Jesus as broken, needy, and without a Shepherd. I started to ask God to reach his sheep, and then I began partnering with him in that task in a fuller way. It has taken many years, but my Father in heaven has brought me to the place of contentment.

We read in the book of Hebrews, "Let us be grateful for receiving a kingdom that cannot be shaken. . . . Be content with what you have, for he has said, 'I will never leave you nor forsake you'" (Hebrews 12:28; 13:5). I have found this to be true.

22

The House God Builds

⸻

In Southall, London, I stood before a room of Asian women who knew very little about the Bible. Their beautiful saris and Punjabi suits filled the room with bright shades of orange, blue, purple, light green, and pink.

Many of the older women had come to England as brides from Kenya, Uganda, India, and Pakistan. Some were followers of Jesus, some not, but all were interested in learning how to keep their children and grandchildren from being overcome by the English culture. I was there to speak to them about parenting. I wanted them to know that God had a plan for them and their children and that it was a good and wise one. So I began.

GOD HAD A PLAN

I know that you have many plans and dreams as you care for your children and raise them to adulthood. Did you know that God had an even bigger plan when he created human beings?

Before creating man and woman, God had created the world full of beauty and design, establishing seas and creating boundaries for continents; speaking sun, stars, moon, and galaxies into existence; separating light from darkness; creating animals without number, fish of all kinds, and plants for food. Then, when all this was in place, he created man from the dust of the earth and breathed into him the breath of life. It was the crowning glory of God's creation.

God gave the man a name, Adam. He gave him work to do, food to eat, and a beautiful world to enjoy. After a time God saw that Adam needed a partner to share life with him. The animals were just not enough. He caused a deep sleep to come over the man and from his rib formed a woman, Eve, a suitable partner for him. They were perfect and so was their life. They lived in a beautiful garden and walked and talked with their Creator in the cool of the day.

There was one prohibition. There was a tree in the middle of the garden: the Tree of the Knowledge of Good and Evil. From this tree they were not allowed to eat. If they did, they would die. Only one restriction—why? God's plan was to create a race of people who would love and serve him because of who he was. The tree was the test. If they failed the test, they would die.

In this garden were trees with every kind of fruit to enjoy, animals to name, and, best of all, a delightful friendship with God. But into this garden of beauty came an enemy of God, a Serpent, with words of doubt: "Did God actually say, 'You shall not eat of any tree in the garden?'" (Genesis 3:1). From Eve's answer one can tell that she had already looked at the forbidden tree, thought about it, and made a judgment about God. She said, "God said, 'You shall not eat of the fruit of the tree . . . neither shall you touch it, lest you die'" (3:3). God had never said they couldn't touch it; only that they could not eat from it.

Having cast doubts on God's command and his goodness, the Serpent told Eve, "You will not surely die. . . . Your eyes will be opened, and you will be like God, knowing good and evil" (3:4–5). Why did he come to her with those words? Why wasn't Adam enough for Eve? Why wasn't God enough?

I wonder if she thought like this: "To be like God, maybe even to be wiser than God—what a heady thought! Why do I have to do what God says? Why can't I be in control, an independent woman?" I don't know if those were her thoughts, but I do know that if I had been there, I would have eaten the fruit—wanting to control my own life, to be my own person with no one telling me what to do. Eve followed her impressions over her instructions. She ate, gave the fruit to her husband, and he ate too.

In one act of disobedience they became rebels against God's love and authority. From then on, the human race was enmeshed in a growing web of corruption and violence.[1] They were ashamed. Now they did not want God in their lives—they hid when he sought their friendship. Now they were afraid. They became blame shifters: Adam blaming his wife, and Eve blaming the Serpent. What a sorry end to such a beautiful beginning.

NOW GOD HAD A PROBLEM

God, who is holy and righteous, who wanted to create a people who would enjoy him, worship him, and serve him, now had two people who were sinners, cut off by one thankless, faithless act of disobedience. He goes into action: the Serpent is cursed, the ground is cursed. Eve will endure pain in childbearing, and Adam would now find work painful because thorns and thistles will grow on the land. Adam and Eve had to leave the garden; when they died, for they would eventually die, they would return to the dust from which they had been formed. All their children would be born with a sinful nature, just like the one Adam and Eve now had. This would have been a sad ending *if* God had not had a plan.

God's curse on his enemy the Serpent amazingly included a promise. "I will put enmity between you and the woman, and between your offspring and her offspring; he shall bruise your head, and you shall bruise his heel" (Genesis 3:15).

War was now declared. Through the centuries God would establish and preserve a people who would belong to him, and the Enemy would do all he could to destroy God's plan and people. God's will was that his beloved Son, Jesus, would finally defeat Satan on the cross by paying for our sins, canceling the debt we owed, and disarming Satan's power to destroy the church. The story begins in the garden, and years later Jesus wins the battle according to plan.

I HAD A PLAN

I knew the Bible. I knew God's instructions on how to train children. I knew his promises too, and so I went to work. Together, my husband and I taught our five children to obey and have good manners. We sent them to Christian schools, played with them, read the Bible to them, and took them to church with us on Sunday. We had an awesome task before us because our children were close in age and came early in our marriage. But our children learned manners, did well in school, did their duties at home, and learned the stories of the Bible.

I HAD A PROBLEM

Outwardly, we were a model family. Training and teaching our children was not wrong, but I assumed it would change their hearts. It did not. We learned this in a very dramatic and humbling way when our daughter Barbara became angry at us when she was eighteen. She said she wanted nothing more to do with us, with God, or with church. My response was to be angry, confused, and afraid. There was nothing I could do. Before this I had always had a plan; now I was faced with a daughter who did not fit the plan—who actually rebelled against it.

What had happened? Didn't I do everything right? Well, yes, outwardly I did, but I forgot the issues of the heart—ours and Barbara's. Without Christ in control, "the heart is deceitful above all things, and desperately wicked" (Jeremiah 17:9 KJV). I had forgotten this, or maybe I had never learned it in the first place.

PSALM 127: GOD'S GOOD AND WISE PLAN

Barbara's rebellion shaped the next eight years of her life and ours. This is when I learned to trust and pray through a song written by King Solomon—Psalm 127. Its words were a marked contrast to the struggles of my soul.

> Unless the LORD builds the house,
>   those who build it labor in vain.
> Unless the LORD watches over the city,
>   the watchman stays awake in vain.
> It is in vain that you rise up early
>   and go late to rest,

eating the bread of anxious toil;
  for he gives to his beloved sleep.
Behold, children are a heritage from the LORD,
  the fruit of the womb a reward.
Like arrows in the hand of a warrior
  are the children of one's youth.
Blessed is the man
  who fills his quiver with them!
He shall not be put to shame
  when he speaks with his enemies in the gate. (Psalm 127)

Unless the LORD builds the house, those who build it labor in vain (v. 1). As I sought to understand what had happened with Barbara, slowly I began to see that it had been my effort, my demands, my control, and my will that had been building my house. If I did all the "right" things, then (I thought) God was obligated to honor my efforts.

Unless the LORD watches over the city, the watchman stays awake in vain (v. 1). This doesn't mean we should do away with watchmen; it means we should realize that we must trust in God to keep a family and a city from evil.

It is in vain that you rise up early and go late to rest, eating the bread of anxious toil; for he gives to his beloved sleep (v. 2). Fear had taken control of me, and I could not quiet my anxiety. What was the next step for me?

Children are a heritage from the LORD, the fruit of the womb a reward. Like arrows in the hands of a warrior are the children of one's youth. Blessed is the man [or woman] who fills his quiver with them! He shall not be put to shame when he speaks with his enemies in the gate (vv. 3–5). It was not easy to give up control, but God brought me to the place where I could believe this last promise.

Several years after Barbara left us, we returned from a difficult trip to Uganda. We called Barbara, and I told her how hard it had been for me to live there. I said, "I was like an orphan." There was a pause at the other end of the line, and then she said, "Mom, that is the way I am too." These were probably the first honest words we had spoken to each other. A few months later, she came back home. Two orphans had come to rest in God—in his faithfulness, his forgiveness, his love. Barbara is now married with four children. We have lived together for more than twenty-five years, two daughters finding rest in the Father's love.

When I finished my talk, the women were silent. Then one said, "I never heard anything like this before." I looked around at these dear women and saw that we were no different from one another. Beneath all our cultural differences, we wanted control, we desired our children to follow in our footsteps, and we needed the reassuring words of this psalm—that God builds the house. The things God taught me so many years ago were now being offered to mothers from places I had never been. Those truths reached their hearts as God continued his work of seeking and redeeming his own.

23

A Kingdom That
Cannot Be Shaken

On Christmas Day 2004, a couple arrived at Thailand's Khao Lake resort to enjoy dinner with a large group of friends. The next day they walked along the beach under a clear blue sky. They took pictures of a tranquil sea, oblivious to the large wave that was forming a line across the horizon. They continued to take pictures as the wave got closer. These were the last five minutes of John and Jackie's lives. Then the tsunami arrived, killing them and more than 230,000 other people.

Their camera was found and their pictures developed to tell the story of this couple's last hours. All who died that day were standing on the brink of eternity and did not know it. All of us here are involved with people who are standing on the brink of eternity and do not know it.

A SHAKEN WORLD

At this moment God is shaking the world. Many of us have lost money. There is an oil well in the Gulf of Mexico that cannot be contained, threatening tourism and wildlife on the Gulf Coast. A volcano in Iceland is spewing ash, and winds carrying that ash are disrupting the airline industry of Europe. In addition, earthquakes in China, Chile, and Haiti have taken thousands of lives. Greece is in serious debt, shaking financial markets around the world.

Some of our missionaries cannot be with us because their lives have also been shaken. There are Social Security issues that disrupt family and ministry, health issues and heart-rending problems with children. If I could sit down with each of you, I would hear stories of how life in a foreign land—learning another language, settling children, learning daily how to love one another and the lost people God brings into your lives—shakes your lives too. This is why it is so important to believe with an unshakable trust that we have a kingdom that cannot be shaken.

For many of us, our world is shaped around our children. Their misbehavior can easily shake us. But there is a kingdom that our children belong to that cannot be shaken.

In 1953, Jack and I moved to Philadelphia from California so that Jack could attend Westminster Seminary. We had three children under the age of three. I heard a sermon on Psalm 127 that children were a heritage of the Lord. It came to me vividly that at this time in my life, God was going to build his kingdom through my family. My heart was filled with joy and faith that this was God's calling—to be in partnership with him. We lived in a second-floor apartment on Jack's part-time salary. A few months later, I was pregnant again, but the truth that I was part of a kingdom that cannot be shaken sustained me through cold winters, children's sickness, and another pregnancy.

Fast-forward forty-three years. We were in Spain, and Jack's heart was failing after major surgery. Though I begged God to keep him alive to lead the mission he loved, I knew he was dying. Very quietly I sensed God speaking to me. "Rose Marie, are you willing for me to take Jack if this is the way for my kingdom to go forward in your family and in the mission?" Through my tears I said Yes. The next morning, Jack arrived in his heavenly home to be welcomed by the One he loved and served.

A SHAKEN LIFE

There have been many heartaches and losses since the day I heard that sermon on Psalm 127 and was filled with joy at being a partner in God's kingdom. I started this talk with the tsunami because such things have gotten me thinking about what it means to have a kingdom that cannot be shaken. When Jack died in 1996, it was as if a tsunami had overtaken me. Wave after wave of grief, sorrow, and loneliness swept over me.

I had to ask myself, "Who am I?" Once I had been Jack's wife; we spoke together, traveled together, and prayed together. Now I felt like an exile. But I had more than a camera left behind. I had a life, and that life needed to be lived. In my grief I struggled to make myself happy and productive. God's goal was to make me like Christ and to bear fruit in old age. He wanted me to learn compassion on a much deeper level—and not through Jack. He wanted me to learn it through a deeper trust in Christ, seeking to help move his kingdom out to the nations, relying on the Holy Spirit as a partner, relying on a King and a kingdom that cannot be shaken.

Through the years there have been many circumstances that shook my world. The things I learned about sonship were things

I learned out of desperate need, in my marriage, my family, and my time in Uganda, to name a few. Many times the Spirit taught with great insight and authority: how to keep a good conscience, the importance of being a forgiving woman every day, trusting in the finished work of Christ to make me holy and content, and the all-important lesson of learning to live as a daughter, not an orphan. Through these tumultuous years Jack and I became partners in God's work of moving his kingdom forward into the world. We encouraged others to come with us—to join the party!

DEATH LEADS TO LIFE

After Jack died, I waited for the same kind of powerful teaching, and what I heard was, "Unless a grain of wheat falls into the earth and dies, it remains alone; but if it dies, it bears much fruit. Whoever loves his life loses it, and whoever hates his life in this world will keep it for eternal life" (John 12:24–25). I did not want to be a single seed, neither did I want to die to bear fruit. I cried myself to sleep many nights with that verse ringing in my ears.

How strange that even in nature, we are reminded that dying goes before life. Every year in England when spring comes, thousands of bulbs that have "died" during the fall and winter produce beautiful yellow daffodils that cover the green parks.

But is dying easy? In the garden Jesus pleads with his Father to let the cup pass. This was the cup of suffering, the cup of his Father's wrath, the cup of being cut off from his Father's love, the cup of becoming sin, the cup of dying—losing his life that we might live. He died that we might not live for ourselves but for a King and a kingdom that cannot be shaken.

There is a kind of death involved in being a missionary.

When I first came to England to live and work among Asians, I truly did not know what I was doing. Lots of times, I still don't know. I live and work among men and women whose language, culture, traditions, food, and way of life are foreign to me. I have learned how to build friendships, but I still need to lean heavily on God.

REMEMBERING GOD'S STORY

I think I had so many insecurities because I had forgotten God's story—his call to Abraham to leave his home, his promise to make Abraham a great nation, his promise that all the families of the earth would be blessed through him. The gospel of the kingdom includes the remaking of the whole world. Gradually, through years of learning about God's kingdom agenda to bring a broken world to himself and as a result of personally reaching out to lonely and needy people, my heart has become more deeply rooted in God's story.

As you read through the Old Testament, you will find that nothing stops God's plan and purpose. Evil does not, the foolishness of men does not, and the sins of God's people do not. For this I am profoundly thankful. My husband wrote, "God wants to and can use us in spite of our sin and weakness, because this is his mission, and he provides the grace we need." This is what I continue to learn.

We are reminded in Hebrews that throughout history men and women through faith "conquered kingdoms, enforced justice, obtained promises, stopped the mouths of lions, quenched the power of fire ... put foreign enemies to flight" (Hebrews 11:33–34). They are our "cloud of witnesses." Therefore, we are to "lay aside every weight, and sin which clings so closely, and . . . run with endurance the race that is set before us." We are told to look to Jesus, "the founder and perfecter of our faith, who . . . endured the cross" so that we do not "grow weary or fainthearted" (Hebrews 12:1–3). "Therefore let us be grateful for receiving a kingdom that cannot be shaken, and thus let us offer to God acceptable worship, with reverence and awe, for our God is a consuming fire" (Hebrews 12:28–29).

AN UNSHAKABLE KINGDOM

"How do you measure the strength of your house?" This question was asked at the funeral of a young mother, who strengthened her house with the unshakable conviction that her children would not live off her faith but learn to trust in the living God for their lives.

God is committed to shake the earth and in the future, the heavens, in order that only the things that cannot be shaken would remain. Anything we place our faith in besides Christ and his kingdom will be shaken. What happens then? Fear, anxiety, depression, and worry take the place of faith. We are told again and again to "fix our eyes not on what is seen, but on what is unseen. For what is seen is temporary, but what is unseen is eternal" (2 Corinthians 4:18 NIV).

We have a kingdom that cannot be shaken because

- We have a King who destroyed the works of the Evil One on the cross.
- We have a King who took the curse for us; who became sin that we might not endure God's wrath.

- We have a King whose blood covers all our failures, insecurities, wandering hearts, lukewarmness, deceit, pride, and unbelief.
- We have a King who rules and reigns, interceding for us.
- We have a King who is preparing a place for us.
- We have a King who says that all things work together for good.

The same Jesus who is now ruling in heaven was the one who

- Stopped a funeral to bring back a widow's son;
- Touched lepers and healed the blind;
- Cast out demons;
- Defended the weak, the needy, and the outcast;
- Healed a destitute woman when she touched his garment;
- Reminded us that his kingdom, like a pearl of great price, is worth selling all to buy;
- Taught us that the kingdom starts small like a mustard seed and is always growing, like yeast expanding dough;
- Taught us that he would take care of the weeds as they grew in a field of wheat.

Why do we need a kingdom that cannot be shaken? We need to remember that there is a kingdom bigger than our own pathetic attempts at kingdom building. Either we are self-confident, self-righteous, self-centered, with too much trust in our abilities, plans, and programs. Or, in the opposite case, if we lack these abilities, we compare ourselves with others and despair. This also reflects our desire to build our own kingdom. When we pray, "Thy kingdom come" (Matthew 6:10 KJV) we are asking God to overthrow our kingdom building and all other kingdoms so that *his* kingdom and *his* kingship will be glorified.

GOD'S KINGDOM IN OUR HEARTS

In London I live in a busy household. This spring there were eleven of us living together for a time. It is a great place to be, but so often I face deep longings—not necessarily for heaven, but for comfort, space, a close friend, a good book. Writing in my journal, I had a question for God: "Is that asking too much?" A few weeks later, my joy was gone. My teaching in Hebrews and 1 Kings was not connecting with my heart or with the women I taught. I had too little love. Add to the mix sickness and a failure to show love in several email exchanges. In that low place, I now wanted God to change my longings. I asked for humility that comes from wisdom, a heart that knows how to love with sincerity, and a faith that expects the Holy Spirit to speak to me through the Word and apply it to all the circumstances of my life.

I wondered whether it is possible to let God's kingdom control us rather than being controlled by worries, cares, duties, disappointments, grief, and sorrows.

When I was halfway through writing this talk, I wasn't feeling well, but Nazma and I had an appointment to have tea together at Harrow-on-the Hill, where there is a famous boys' school. Nazma is a convert from Islam and deeply burdened for her family. She is the only believer in her extended family. She asked how I was doing. I started to choke up and said, "I am working on a talk that reminds me of my husband. I will be with a large group of people who knew him, and I am sad." As I talked, she listened, and soon the burden lifted. We talked about how often we prayed for one another and God lifted our burdens. I came to her weak, and she responded in faith. When I speak I recruit a host of people to pray for me. Through many hard times, I have reached out in my need and asked people to pray—for my heart to be restored, for my vision to be refocused so that I am not seduced from a simple and pure devotion to Christ. God continues to answer those prayers.

At Christmas in 2004 Victor Amaranath and his family were on holiday in Sri Lanka. It was their first visit in nineteen years. On the 26th they were planning to spend the day on the white sandy beach. They were packed up and ready to go when three-year-old Lydia, the youngest of five children, was bitten by a dog on her face and had to be rushed to the hospital. It was a terrifying experience for the whole family, but they did not go to the beach that day—the day the tsunami struck. As Victor told me this story he said, "God protected our family." He now works for WHM in London.

We have a kingdom that cannot be shaken. Our flesh and the Evil One will cause us to doubt this truth when the hard times come, but do not forget what Jesus said to his disciples, who really messed things up: "Fear not, little flock, for it is your Father's good pleasure to give you the kingdom" (Luke 12:32).

The shakings will come. Dying is part of living, suffering and trials are part of life, but do not fix your eyes or heart on them. God's kingdom agenda is to fix every broken thing and bring all under his saving rule. We are all part of his story. God has done more than I could ask or think in my family and in WHM. Today we are all living proof of his faithfulness.

EPILOGUE

G od, the Consummate Gardener, had a lot of work to do when he started with me. A garden locked up needed to be unlocked, and a fountain sealed needed to be opened. The North wind blew and did its work. The winds of failure, sickness, death, weakness, disappointments, hurts, rejection, loneliness, weariness, confusion, and ambiguities were a part of daily life.

Through the years I tended to forget that he was always at work, breaking up the ground of a hardened heart; removing rocks of unbelief and pride; pulling up weeds of anxiety, deceit, and worry; and cutting down trees of ambition, self-sufficiency, and self-righteousness so that the sun could nourish the plants. What I could never have done for myself, God did for me.

GOD'S GARDENS

In the beginning, God created a world full of beauty and planted a special garden for Adam and Eve, the crown of his creation. He loved to walk with them in the cool of the day, giving them every fruit to eat but one. Into this garden came an Enemy to cast doubts on God's word, his love, and his purpose. He tempted Eve to eat, and both she and Adam succumbed to his lies.

Through the years, I too have listened to the seductive temptations of the Enemy: "You are alone; you are a failure; God does not love like he says he does; he is keeping you from real happiness." I found that Satan always accuses, forever spins out a dark future, and cuts me off from grace, forgiveness, and mercy.

But there was another garden, where Jesus agonized with tears of blood as he anticipated being separated from his Father's love, facing his rejection and wrath, taking on the ugliness of the world's sin, and dying on a cruel cross. On the cross, finally, the Enemy was defeated. His hold was broken. A fountain of blood was opened for the cleansing of sin. The record of my sins was cancelled, the debt was paid, and Satan was disarmed. God forgave our sins, "cancelling the record of debt that stood against us with its legal demands. This he set aside, nailing it to the cross" (Colossians 2:14–15). Here the God of the impossible is fully revealed.

Now God is building a much bigger garden; it is becoming a kingdom for his glory. I am deeply thankful that I have a place in his kingdom. I have an ever-growing confidence that the Gardener is still at work, digging, planting, watering, and harvesting. I keep a journal, and looking back over the last few months of writing, I am reminded again of why the Gardener still has work to do.

This is an entry written on July 18, 2010: "I am heartily sick of motivation that goes no further than duty and obligation—it is my default mode."

September 28, 2010: "Aunt B not eating, paperwork for nursing home stalled, not able to get to the writing. I am an impatient woman—I do not like hemming in or slowing down. I tend to think of circumstances as isolated from God, but all the ups and down of yesterday were *sent* by God. God must deal with my heart. I must not try to change what I cannot—especially my own heart."

The next day, after reading Micah 6:8 I wrote: "'What does the Lord require: To walk humbly with your God.' This I cannot do because pride deceives me. I need your help for that which I cannot do. God says he will have compassion; he will cast our sins into the depths of the sea. This is truly all I can depend on. I cannot make myself humble or right. I keep moving away from the humble place to getting back on the throne, and the only one who sits there is God."

There are more examples, but these are enough to show that if my heart is not filled with Christ and his purposes, I will be self-centered and self-righteous. I will live and work out of pride, not humility.

LOOKING AHEAD

God's story in my life continues as I live in a household of eight in London. When there are parties, I am part of the team that welcomes our guests. I help with laundry, listen, learn, and pray. I teach in our weekly Bible study. I listen to the heartbreaking stories of Asian women whose children are making foolish choices. I laugh and sometimes cry in our study as we share our hearts with one another. I pray with a friend whose extended family excludes her because of her faith in Christ. When I take a cab, I talk to my Asian driver about why it is important to place his faith in Jesus as Lord.

This life is not the end. I look forward to seeing another river and another tree: "Then the angel showed me the river of the water of life, bright as crystal, flowing from the throne of God and of the Lamb through the middle of the street of the city; also, on either side of the river, the tree of life with its twelve kinds of fruit, yielding its fruit each month. The leaves of the tree were for the healing of the nations" (Revelation 22:1–2).

Nothing is impossible with God. He is making all things new.

NOTES

Chapter 1

1. Martin Luther, *A Commentary on Saint Paul's Epistle to the Galatians* (Grand Rapids: Baker, 1979), xxiv.

Chapter 2

1. Mary Lou Cummings, *Surviving Without Romance: African Women Tell Their Stories* (Scottsdale, Pa.: Herald, 1991) 134–138.

Chapter 3

1. "The Harvester," published by World Harvest Mission, 1999.
2. Richard F. Lovelace, *Dynamics of Spiritual Life* (Downers Grove, Ill.: InterVarsity Press, 1979), 131.

Facing Loss, Finding Life

1. Author paraphrase. Augustine, Saint, Bishop of Hippo, *The Confessions of St. Augustine,* Rosalie A. de Rossett, ed., (Chicago, IL: Moody Press, 1981), 22–23.

Chapter 4

1. John Wimber, "Spirit Song," Mercy/Vineyard, 1979.

Chapter 5

1. Patricia St. John, *Patricia St. John Tells Her Own Story* (Carlisle, Cumbria UK: OM Publishing, 1995), xii.
2. C. S. Lewis, *The Great Divorce* (New York: Macmillan, 1963), 23.
3. Lewis, *Great Divorce*, 72.

Chapter 7

1. Patricia St. John, *Until the Day Breaks: The Life and Work of Lilias Trotter* (Bromley, Kent, UK: OM Publishing; Loughborough, Leics, UK: Arab World Ministries, 1990), 60–61.
2. R. Arthur Mathews, *Born for Battle* (Bromley, Kent, UK: OM Publishing 1978), 166.
3. C. John Miller, *Outgrowing the Ingrown Church* (Grand Rapids: Zondervan, 1986), 53.

Learning to Pray

1. O. Hallesby, *Prayer*, trans. Clarence J. Carlsen (Minneapolis: Augsburg, 1931), 21.
2. Miriam Huffman Rockness, comp. and ed., *A Blossom in the Desert: Reflections of Faith in the Art and Writings of Lilias Trotter* (Grand Rapids: Discovery House, 2007), 65.
3. C. John Miller, *The Heart of a Servant Leader*, ed. Barbara Miller Juliani (Phillipsburg, N.J.: P & R, 2004), 47.
4. Miller, *Heart of a Servant Leader*, 48.

Chapter 8

"Entering God's Presence with Prayer," was taken from a talk given in May 2001 at Harvey Cedars (New Jersey) Bible Conference.

1. Hallesby, *Prayer*, 64.
2. David Foster Estes, *International Standard Bible Encyclopedia*, Online Bible, v. 4.1: http://www.bible-history.com/isbe/
3. Kenneth E. Bailey, *Poet and Peasant and Through Peasant Eyes:*

A Literary–Cultural Approach to the Parables in Luke (Grand
Rapids: Wm. B. Eerdmans, 1983), 120.

4. Hallesby, *Prayer,* 64.

Chapter 9

"Groaning and Glory," consists of material originally presented at
World Harvest Mission's London Prayer Conferences. Participants
were preparing to go on prayer walks throughout the Southhall
area of London, where WHM ministers to the expatriate Asian
community.

1. N. T. Wright, *The Crown and the Fire: Meditations on the Cross
   and the Life of the Spirit* (Grand Rapids: Wm. B. Eerdmans,
   1992), 89.

2. Hallesby, *Prayer,* 20.

Chapter 11

"Kingdom Praying: In Step with the Spirit," is comprised of material
presented at a Sonship seminar in India in 2009.

1. J. H. Oldham, *Florence Allshorn and the Story of St. Julian's*
   (London: Hodder & Stoughton, 1951), 35.

2. Tom Wright, *Matthew for Everyone: Part Two* (London: SPCK,
   2002), 161.

Chapter 12

1. R. Kent Hughes, *Ephesians: The Mystery of the Body of Christ*
   (Wheaton, Ill.: Crossway, 1990), 117.

2. James W. Hewitt, ed. *Illustrations Unlimited* (Wheaton, Ill.:
   Tyndale, 1988), 321.

Chapter 13

1. John Piper, "Why a Conference Commission on Prayer?" August
   10, 1988, *www.desiringGod.org/resource-library/articles/why-a
   -conference-commission-on-prayer* (June 11, 2011).

2. St. John, *Until the Day Breaks,* 118.

3. Mathews, *Born for Battle*, 12.

4. Mathews, *Born for Battle*, 13.

5. Sinclair Ferguson, *Taking the Christian Life Seriously* (Grand Rapids: Zondervan, 1981).

6. N. T. Wright, *Following Jesus: Biblical Reflections on Discipleship* (London: SPCK, 1994), 61–62.

7. Wright, *Following Jesus*, 105.

Chapter 14

1. Cleland B. McAfee, "Near to the Heart of God," 1903.

2. Carl F. H. Henry, consulting ed., *The Biblical Expositor*, 3 vols. (Grand Rapids: Baker Book House, 1960), 2:39.

3. Derek Kidner, *Psalms 73—150* (Downers Grove, Ill.: InterVarsity Press, 1973), 466.

Chapter 16

"Eve Believed an Impossible Lie," was taken from a talk given in 2000 and includes the themes covered in our conference in India.

1. Derek Kidner, *Genesis: An Introduction and Commentary* (Downers Grove, Ill.: InterVarsity Press, 1967), 68.

2. Alister McGrath, *Why Does God Allow Suffering?* (London: Hodder & Stoughton, 1992), 21.

3. Barbara Juliani, November 3, 1999.

Chapter 18

1. C. S. Lewis, *The Lion, the Witch and the Wardrobe* (New York: Macmillan, 1950; Collier edition, 1970), 75–76.

2. Samuel Rutherford to Lady Boyd, paraphrased.

3. McGrath, *Why Does God Allow Suffering*, 24, 29.

4. Charles H. Spurgeon, "A Woman of a Sorrowful Spirit," Sermon No. 1515. Delivered at the Metropolitan Tabernacle, Newington. *http://www.spurgeongems.org/vols25–27/chs1515.pdf*.

5. McGrath, *Why Does God Allow Suffering*, 46.